THE
COMPOSITE
PERSUASION

JOEL MARSH

www.joelmarsh.com

2011

Printed in the United States of America.

For information, contact the author online: www.joelmarsh.com

Designed by Joel Marsh.

Marsh, Joel, 1980–

      The Composite Persuasion / Joel Marsh—1st ed.

      Includes bibliographical references.

      ISBN 978-1-4709-2828-5

      1. Persuasion. 2. Motivation. 3. Psychology. 4. Business.

Originally published in paperback by the author.

CONTENTS

THE
COMPOSITE
PERSUASION

Preface

Read this first.

THIS BOOK STARTED AS A GUT FEELING AND QUICKLY BECAME A MONSTER.

My official job title is Experience Architect.

I literally design experiences. I am a specialist in the digital world, responsible for optimizing websites, software, and digital products. When I am done with something it is easier to use, more appealing, and makes more money.

If you are anything like me, you find people interesting. You might watch the crowd when you have lunch at the mall or sip coffee at a café. You might keep track of people on Facebook a little more than you should or enjoy reality television a little more than you admit. Ah, guilty pleasures.

I do all of these things and I am willing to wager that you do too, given the chance. Don't worry, your secret is safe with me.

Human behavior is also a huge part of what I do for a living. Applying it in a practical way can be crucial. In some cases a good Experience Architect can add millions of dollars in revenue by changing a few simple details. I have experienced this myself and it is a very empowering feeling.

Several years ago, for the sake of professional self-improvement, I began looking for books and studies about predictable 'people stuff': decision-making, getting people to agree, favorite colors...whatever. Patterns I could use.

I just wanted more people to click the "join now" button.

The Internet is comparatively new so when I was unable to find good information within my field I went to the usual suspects: sales, marketing, and psychology. I found good tips and principles there, but again, not a lot that I could apply directly.

Common sense told me that experts who profit from persuasion might have some good ideas. A gut feeling told me that persuasion did not depend on context as much as on commonality among people. So I began to seek out persuaders in hopes of stealing some of their tricks.

As my search for persuasive methods spiralled outward I began reading about subjects as disparate as criminal interrogation, fortune-telling, pick-up artists and on and on. Over 40 persuasive disciplines in total. Although no individual disciplines provided a solid "persuasion method" I began to notice patterns and connections between seemingly unrelated methods. Hidden under the industry-specific jargon, these people were independently discovering the same thing over and over.

Eventually persuasion became an obsession. Hundreds of books; weeks' worth of audio; days upon days of video; inestimable online content; journal articles; and research from a long list of communication disciplines. Not to mention the vast amount of research done by the expert authors who created the books, audio, video, and articles that I had assimilated.

Originally, I had no intention of writing a book. My research was purely for my own improvement and success. Moreover, my industry measures everything down to minute details, so if my research didn't work with specific scenarios, it would have been worth nothing. Ironically, that may be the reason this book exists; I was looking for a method, not book material.

After consuming so much material about persuasive techniques, I noticed something peculiar: there are very few books about persuasion itself, but lots of "persuasion books".

Some persuasion books come from authors who have ventured boldly into the field – which is what social scientists call real-life – in search of elusive examples of real persuasion. They observe and report and we all read about ourselves with unbridled fascination.

Other persuasion books recount the vast experience from expert persuaders such as ex-FBI agents or master negotiators, using the various methods of their trade. These cunning tactics allow us to gain friends or up-sell our customers just as the author would.

And finally, some persuasion books provide us with the principles on which persuasion supposedly works, so we can better understand and explain persuasive scenarios in our lives. Their carefully-chosen anecdotes demonstrate the principles in real situations so we might learn from them.

These books are often interesting enough, perhaps useful enough, and occasionally insightful enough to affect us in our daily lives.

However, none of those books are about persuasion itself.

All of those books are about *people being persuasive*.

The experience of one person in "the field" is never enough to describe every human everywhere, and at best it is only enough to create broad stereotypes.

It is inherently true that an expert must know a lot about a narrow field of knowledge, and therefore their experience becomes a *metaphor* for our lives, rather than instructions.

Vague principles are nice, but once we begin to apply those to a specific situation we quickly realize how little we have actually learned from principled, anecdotal persuasion books.

Marketers, for example, are famous for phrasing tactics in language that describes nothing, such as the phrase "social proof" (demonstrating that other people like something too) used famously in Robert Cialdini's book *Influence: The Psychology of Persuasion*. It sounds like something concrete, but when you actually turn to your team and say "we need to create social proof", they still ask "how?" More importantly, when it doesn't work, we're lost for an explanation.

Ultimately, none of these books teach persuasion in a reliable way; they merely tell stories with persuasion as a common thread. Very entertaining; not so helpful.

This is not one of those books. This book is a meta-study.

A meta study is "a study of studies". This book is a meta study that brings together expert research from almost every discipline that involves goal-oriented communication, including (and especially) several unethical practices. We may not agree with what some of these people do with their skills, but we must admit: they are damn good at it.

The result of that meta-research is possibly the most comprehensive explanation of persuasive tactics and concepts ever compiled, in a step-by-step format – a "composite" persuasion method.

I have chosen a non-academic format for this book, so you won't see footnotes and tons of references throughout the text. This book is written for everyone, as all research should be.

DISCIPLINES INCLUDED

Disciplines considered and overlapped during the research for this book include:

1. Advertising
2. Animal Training
3. Body Language
4. Brainwashing
5. CIA Spy Training
6. Cold Reading / "Fortune Telling"
7. Copywriting
8. Conflict Style Inventories
9. Criminal Interrogation
10. Criminal Profiling
11. Cults & Religion
12. Demographics

13. Evolutionary Science
14. Game Theory
15. Graphic Design
16. Hostage Negotiation
17. Hypnosis
18. Infomercials
19. Interaction Design
20. L.A.B. Profiles
21. Learning
22. Marketing
23. Memory
24. Military Recruiting / Training
25. Negotiation
26. Neuro-Linguistic Programming (NLP)
27. Neuroscience
28. Paralinguistics
29. Personality Theory / Typology
30. Pick-Up / Seduction Arts
31. Psycholinguistics
32. Psychology
(Social, Cognitive, Behavioural, Experimental, Applied, etc.)
33. Psychopolitics
34. Rhetoric
35. Sales
36. Screenplay Writing
37. Song Writing
38. Speechwriting
39. Stand-Up Comedy
40. Teleplay Writing

What I actually discovered among these disciplines was a problem of *specificity*. Expert after expert was so involved with their own specific work that they rarely bothered to check for existing solutions elsewhere.

A similar thing happens, for example, with most people's taste in music.

Ask anyone what type of music they like. The answer is likely to be "I like a lot of music" or "I like almost everything."
But ask again.
Say: "Like what, specifically?" and the answer you receive will reveal the deception.

"I like rap, hip-hop, R&B... lots of stuff."
(Urban)

"I like country, western, some bluegrass."
(Country)

"Anything I can dance to, like techno, house, trance..."
(Electronic)

"I like the classics, Blue Oyster Cult, ELO, Zeppelin."
(Classic Rock)

"I like all the greats: Bach, Wagner, Mozart."
(Classical)

"I like all the greats: Coltrane, Miles, Armstrong."
(Jazz)

"I like pop and rock and R&B, anything except country."
(Top 40)

In actuality, each of those comments indicate a very narrow section of music. This is not unlike a business person who follows every nuance of their industry, remaining blind to other industries. Or a scientist that is passionate about their field of research while oblivious to research happening elsewhere.

Why would we explore other options when we already have something we like, right?

Exactly.

Like those music-lovers, business people, and scientists, professional persuaders have the same problem.

It is unlikely that marketers would read, discuss, and research methods pertaining to fortune-telling. They have marketing to do! It is also unlikely that a group of hypnotists would sit and learn the craft of songwriting and compare it to their own work. And interrogators would be unlikely to learn about seducing girls in a club.

It is very unlikely that these people would then all work together to see if there were a long list of mutual benefits.

What this book proposes is that all of these people in all of these disciplines are actually studying the same thing. However, since no one was looking for the bigger picture, no one found it. In (French) psychology, this is called *déformation professionnelle*, or professional bias.

Speaking of which, psychologists are obviously interested in persuasion as well.

Like any academic discipline, there are rules to studying psychology, and true social communication under controlled conditions is something of an oxymoron. Social situations are highly complex, improvisational, and colourful, and more of those characteristics can mean more fun. In other words, the perfect social situation to study is the opposite of a perfect clinical experiment.

The Catch-22 is that practical persuasion evolves quickly and can even be taught without any idea of why it works, while clinical persuasion evolves very slowly and produces verifiable data. You can become a great salesperson by watching another great salesperson, but proving that in a lab may not be realistic.

The solution: Overlap all the practical disciplines to find out what works, and then consult science to find out why.

During this research, no less than five expert authors were found — in unrelated disciplines — that actually mentioned similarities between another discipline and their own. All were fascinated by the parallel thinking, and then dropped the subject.

Pick-Up Artists (trained seducers) even took it a step further and started incorporating other disciplines into their own. However, due to the counter-intuitive nature of attraction psychology, many of those techniques would backfire if you simply change the genders of the people involved or the setting in which they take place. All of these experts are effective in their own scenarios, and that was the problem. Why explore other options when you like what you have, right?

This is not a book about people being persuasive; it is a book about persuasion, in all its forms. It is not based solely on my experiences, but the experiences of many, many experts. And the persuasive methods described in this book are concrete, reliable, and can be executed by anyone. Needless to say, this book applies to a lot more than websites.

Most importantly, this book is unique in the way that it treats the person being persuaded, whether they are a friend, a stranger, a group, or ourselves. It gives them some credit, assuming they are both a thinking human being and that they are aware of normal social conventions. This book also assumes that if it is true for others, it is true for us. This "human element" was shockingly absent in most reference material I read; notably the scientific literature.

My gut feeling turned out to be more valid than I had imagined: not only did different persuaders have things in common, they were all doing the same thing. They just didn't realize it.

A CAUTIONARY NOTE

All readers should be explicitly informed, warned, and aware that this information is presented as an anthology of knowledge and theory, and that this information is neither positive nor negative until combined with intent.

Some information contained in this book theoretically provides tools to create highly manipulative or emotionally damaging situations. It would be naïve to ignore this fact, and any such behaviour is strictly discouraged. Act ethically and responsibly. Such information is provided for your protection, not for ill-will toward others.

ACKNOWLEDGEMENTS

There were a few influential people during the creation of this book, most of whom helped just by being themselves and by saying the right things at the right times. Hence, their brilliance.

Josh Gold-Smith, talented in both music and journalism, was a catalytic force during my early interest in persuasive patterns, and inadvertently set me on a journey that took over three years to complete.

Peter Brauer was not only my business partner during the early discovery of the 8 universal steps of persuasion, but also gave me different perspectives on many core ideas, sometimes allowing me to realize how they fit together.

Ted Persson, Executive Creative Director of the illustrious Great Works Group, was my employer as this book went to publication. He is not only a brilliant persuader in his own right, but also planted seeds that contributed to this and maybe future books as well.

Martin Sahlberg, a master sales manager, friend, and excellent people-person, gave me invaluable advice and feedback during the editing phase of this book. He far exceeded any expectations I could have had in terms of his interest and contribution.

Mikael Zetterberg, a gifted strategist with a natural intuition for analyzing groups, is one of those people that improves you just because he sits at the next desk. His input was also very valuable during the editing phase.

Camilla Andersson – the love of my life – not only makes my life possible while pursuing these obsessive interests, but also has a talent for asking me simple questions that cause weeks of re-consideration. Socratic method, indeed.

And finally, to the millions of people that have come through my websites and software, unwittingly providing experimental data, and to everyone who has ever persuaded, manipulated, or indoctrinated me in any way, thank you very much!

Introduction

Persuasion, manipulation & brainwashing.

WHAT IS PERSUASION?

WHAT IS MANIPULATION?

WHAT IS BRAINWASHING?

These can be difficult questions.

Depending on who you ask, you may receive varying answers, and you may even have varying opinions of your own. In actuality they are the same. This book deals with all three.

We will define *persuasion* as an exchange between two parties, where one or both parties will benefit, and neither party's situation will become worse. In other words, a "win-win" situation.

For example, when a patient visits a therapist with a goal to quit smoking, it is in the therapist's best interest to help the patient so that he can not only earn a fee, but so that the patient will be satisfied, return for help with other issues, and spread positive word-of-mouth about the therapist. The patient may pay for the service, but they receive a benefit in exchange. The therapist may try to stretch the therapy over a few sessions to maximize his fee, but regardless of the therapist's method and ethics the patient must successfully quit smoking for the persuasion to be a success. Everybody wins.

A hostage negotiator enters a tense situation with the goal of persuading a violent criminal to release the hostages without harm. The negotiator may want to achieve a promotion, or the glory of press coverage, or impress the attractive new trainee, but regardless of whether his goal is "pure", he must do good rather than evil for the persuasion to be a success.

A songwriter and her record label may use a tried, tested, and true songwriting formula to create an addictively catchy song – with fame and fortune in mind – but in order for the persuasion to succeed we must love the song when we hear it.

All of these are positive gains for the person being persuaded – regardless of the intent of the persuader – and that can be called persuasion, as opposed to manipulation or brainwashing.

Manipulation, as far as this book is concerned, is a situation in which the manipulator gains at the expense of the manipulated. A "win-lose" situation.

For example, when a drug dealer provides a depressed friend with a free dose of his wares, it may appear to be an act of selfless generosity, but the resulting addiction is the actual goal. In order for the manipulation to succeed, the manipulated person has to become addicted to the drug. Interestingly, because the dealer is then the source of withdrawal relief, he is not hated for creating the addiction (as he should be), but followed religiously until the addiction can be cured.

Similarly, a cult leader and his disciples will always approach new potential recruits under the guise of friendship and charity; they provide meals, trips, and unconditional social acceptance, seemingly from the sheer goodness of their hearts. Once the person has accepted this gift from the cult leader they are quickly and efficiently transformed into a loyal follower of the faith using techniques explained in this book. It is not the gift that makes them loyal, but the subsequent manipulative efforts. The cult leader clearly has no intention of providing the benefit for free, but that only becomes clear when it is already too late. For the manipulation to succeed the manipulated person has to become a follower of the cult leader's cult. Although, if we were to ask the cult leader, they would invariably say this was persuasion, not manipulation.

A child who wants candy or toys may cry and thrash around on the floor, or even sulk and refuse to show signs of love toward the parent because the child has learned that this behavior causes submission. Similar to the drug dealer and the cult leader, the child is using the need of the person being manipulated to create agreement. Teenagers in particular can become disturbingly adept and remorseless in their use of guilt, using phrases such as "I hate you," until submission is achieved, and rewarded with "I love you." In order for that manipulation to succeed the parent must feel guilt or frustration and submit to the child's demands. Not the most elegant method, but it works.

Brainwashing is like persuasion and manipulation, but is taken to a wholly immoral and extreme level, where the brainwasher gains immeasurable power and control, while the person being brainwashed is broken and enslaved. The action of the persuader or manipulator is no longer left to chance or coercion, but is forced – sometimes violently – as the only option other than pain and suffering. Effective brainwashing leaves the brainwashed person without the ability to imagine alternative scenarios, as well as becoming fiercely loyal to the brainwasher. Brainwashing is done every day by religions and governments and companies world-wide.

The difference between persuasion, manipulation, and brainwashing is merely the result for the "other person". The methods are the same 8 steps.

If you are interested in persuasion, you are probably more concerned with your personal improvement and the ability to wield social power to gain more friends, lovers, and success. You have waited long enough for good things to happen to you and it is time to tap some of your potential. This book is definitely for you.

If you are interested in manipulation, you have probably been its victim before, maybe even many times. You may be "too trusting". You may be called "gullible" by friends and family, and you want to do something about it. By understanding the methods of your manipulators you can become immune to their ruthless tactics. You may even be able to turn the tables on them. This book is definitely for you, too.

If you are interested in brainwashing then you are probably a megalomaniac, and should seek professional counseling or send me an email, because I might have a job for you as my publicist.

The Composite Persuasion brings together persuasion, manipulation, and brainwashing expertise from a wide range of disciplines, in a step-by-step format that is applicable to any scenario whether moral or immoral, passive or extreme. Regardless of what you want, this book will show you how to get it, but ultimately it will be up to you to actually go out there and do it. Although some people may try to make persuasion, manipulation, and brainwashing sound like distant relatives of one another, they are actually more like triplets. Different, but hard to tell apart.

Persuasion is a word we attach to scenarios where success is seen as competence. Manipulation is associated with scenarios where the persuader is more of an evil-doer. The difference can be a matter of which side you're on, because few people ever refer to themselves as "manipulative". We will refer to all three ideas under the term "persuasion" but do not be naïve about which is which; manipulators love naïve people.

WHY IS PERSUASION IMPORTANT?

Persuasion is all around us. We tend to label things as "persuasive" or "influential" when they involve a lot of people or money or success, but in actuality we are persuaded and persuading all day, every day. Whether you are trying to convince your spouse to drive the kids so you can do something fun, or asking someone to pass the salt, the other person always has the ability to say no. If they say yes, someone has been persuasive. It is important to realize that these mundane situations are persuasive, because these types of situations allow society to function.

Your first reaction may be "yeah but, those things are so simple, why would anyone say no?" And that is a good point, which you should think through a little further.

What if you asked me to pass the salt, and I said no. I would be rude, and you would be without the salt. Who really loses?

Both of us, actually.

It is quite significant to realize that I will probably pass you the salt in order to avoid disrupting the dinner table, and you are so sure that I will agree (even if you haven't realized it) that you would be surprised if I said no.

If I say no, the only thing I really lose is some respect from the people around me, and I will feel ashamed or resentful. That's it! It's only social pressure – a temporary feeling – but it defines a lot of our decisions, every day.

Now imagine if you knew about something that would create social pressure in the same way, but you wanted me to buy a car rather than passing the salt. Perhaps everyone in my neighborhood is getting new cars, and I am being left behind. I will have the same feeling of shame or resentment if I don't do what is "expected".

Suddenly that principle is much more powerful, which makes even little persuasions extremely important to observe.

The really interesting part is that only you benefit when I pass the salt, and I get nothing. I don't *gain* respect for doing what is expected of me. According to our definitions, that's manipulation, not persuasion. The question then becomes, should you feel guilty for using me like that?

Below you will find three brief stories illustrating persuasion in action. They range from commonplace to severe; obvious to nearly invisible; in no particular order. Try to imagine yourself in each situation and how you would think, feel, and react. Keep in mind that each example has happened in real-life millions of times, in cultures around the world, and is irrefutably successful. Pay attention to details and find the persuasive elements. Then we will take each scenario apart and learn how they work in the next chapter.

STORY #1

"THE MAKING OF A HERO"

John was a typical American boy who, like many others, felt unsure about his future as high school graduation approached. Unlike his upper-middle-class friends, his parents were indifferent about his university education, and did not encourage him, despite his uncertainty. John himself wanted to succeed like everyone does, but also wanted freedom from his parents and the town where he lived.

"I didn't go to college, and I turned out just fine," his father said at breakfast one morning, sitting in his grease-stained cover-alls. "Not everybody can be a doctor or a lawyer you know, and there is honor in working with your hands." John had never assumed he would become a doctor or a lawyer.

In the months leading up to graduation, many colleges sent representatives to promote the benefits of choosing their campuses for post-secondary education. This included young officers from the military academy who looked no older than John, but possessed an aura of confidence and perfection like no student. "The Army wants you to be all you can be" they said, and they meant it. Dressed in authoritative, immaculate uniforms, they stood with perfect posture and spoke with a kind, respectful tone to boys and girls like John. It felt like the first time anyone had treated them with respect, and it was definitely the first time anyone had spoken of their potential with sincere optimism. Not only that, they explained exactly how this potential could be realized by joining the Army.

After getting brochures and materials from the officers, John walked away with a sense of pride and ambition for himself and his future; an unfamiliar but welcome feeling. And they were going to pay him to enlist! All the other schools wanted to charge him to learn, those arrogant bastards. He wouldn't be settling for a student loan like all the popular kids; he was making a smart financial decision instead. Finally, someone could see in him what John had known all along.

After his 18th birthday John quickly joined the Army. He was patted on the back and given a tour of the facilities. Everyone in the Army office seemed very welcoming and positive. John had hesitated for a second before signing the contract, but when the officer said "the army isn't for everyone," he took it as a challenge. It was for him. "You've made the right choice," they told him. He agreed. His parents seemed concerned, especially his mother, but the deed was done. He didn't need their permission anyway, he was an adult now, and with his signing bonus in hand he had more money than his father had ever seen in one place.

When he arrived for the first day of boot camp John was lined up with the other new recruits and was introduced to the General. A highly decorated officer, he paced and spoke calmly and firmly about the challenges that lay ahead, the honor that serving their country would bring to them, and how they would be transformed into strong, brave men and women. They would be all they could be. They were standing straighter already.

They were assembled into groups and assigned beds, uniforms, and drill sergeants with systematic precision. The tone of the interactions with superior officers immediately changed from "you are amazing and we are lucky to have you" into "you belong to us and you should be happy I haven't punished you already". Formal procedures were created for every minute of every day, and deviance was punished relentlessly. From the moment they woke up until the time they went to sleep (for only 6 hours per night) they were controlled, measured, and punished for every mistake, and the definition of a mistake was the Army's definition of a mistake. This was how heroes are made, after all.

This training camp happened to exist near a steep hill, and every morning the recruits were told to bring their beds from their sleeping quarters to the top of the hill using only their bare hands. Upon reaching the top of the hill the sergeant would become furious and demand the beds be re-placed and made to perfection, otherwise there would be no lunch. And if they were late, there would be no lunch even if the sheets were perfect.

On the first day the recruits acted out of fear, failed the task, and received no lunch. On the second day they failed again. And again on the third day. Tired from insufficient sleep and hungry from losing lunch privileges, on the fourth day they began working together and succeeded. Lunch that day was the greatest meal they had ever eaten and even the drill sergeant seemed impressed, if only for a moment.

At the conclusion of training John had completely forgotten his desire for individuality, adulthood, and freedom. His life with his parents and in high school seemed distant and irrelevant. His new identity was conditioned to be perfect: follow orders without hesitation and perform tasks with precision and accuracy every time. He no longer accepted the weakness that had allowed him to fail before. He had also shown aptitude during training and was eventually promoted to train future recruits in the exact manner he had been trained.

Several years later, John was called to serve his country as a soldier in the Middle East. There he killed many enemies, led many successful missions, and once – although he would never speak of it to anyone – gave an order that accidentally killed a civilian child.

John's career in the Army lasted 20 years, and he received many awards for his valor and bravery, which were awarded during elaborate ceremonies as his proud parents and fellow soldiers watched with tears in their eyes. He had made something of himself, and would be remembered as a hero.

STORY #2

"THE BEST-SELLING DISASTER OF ALL TIME"

This story begins with a treasure hunt: some scientists are using high-tech mini-submarines to explore a shipwreck, looking for a massive diamond they believe to have gone down with the ship. Upon retrieving a special safe, which they are sure will contain the diamond, they crack it open to find nothing but documents. Little do they know, one of the documents is a charcoal portrait of a girl wearing the exact diamond they are looking for. The portrait is dated April 14th, 1912; the day the Titanic sank.

(If you don't want to find out how it ends, feel free to skip to Story #3)

The oldest living survivor, an elderly woman, is flown to the treasure-hunt to provide what scientists hope will be crucial clues about the diamond's whereabouts.

Soon thereafter we are introduced to Rose Dewitt-Decator, the beautiful young heiress to a fortune and the subject of the portrait, and Jack Dawson, a charming, poor, young man who is only on Titanic in the first place because of a lucky hand in poker. Her family is typically rich, arrogant, southern money, including her fiancé. The year is 1912 and this is Titanic's maiden voyage.

After years of being smothered into the expectations of her social status Rose decides to throw herself from the back railing of the boat. Jack, seeing her climb over the railing, interrupts and explains that he will not enjoy swimming in the painfully cold water when he jumps in to save her. Just as she begins to agree, she slips from the railing and Jack narrowly catches her. However, during the commotion some other first-class passengers come running and misinterpret the situation as Jack having tried to assault Rose. She covers for him, he is silent about her, and everything is resolved. But a romance has begun.

After several minor encounters the sexual tension continues to build and after discovering his talent for art, Rose asks Jack to draw a nude portrait of her – the portrait found in the opening scene.

With Rose's family trying to crush their tumultuous romance and the excruciating sexual tension coming to a climax, Jack and Rose escape from her family into the cargo hold where they make love in a stored car. The ill-fated ship collides with an iceberg immediately after, and begins to sink.

During the crisis with the iceberg Jack is framed for stealing the diamond pendant and is handcuffed to a pipe as the ship continues sinking. At the last minute Rose uses an emergency fire axe to cut Jack free and they race to beat the rising water and get to the upper deck.

The ship goes down and hundreds of people are dumped into the ocean, including Jack and Rose.

When the rescue boat arrives and begin looking for survivors, we discover that during their wait to be rescued Jack has died in the ice-cold water. Rose releases his hand and he sinks slowly into the ocean's depths while Rose swims to a nearby body that has a whistle. After blowing the whistle and attracting the rescue boat, Rose is saved.

We then jump back to present day, as the elderly Rose drops the diamond pendant off the scientists' ship (revealing she had had it with her all along) and goes to sleep. During the night she passes away amidst photos of her doing all the things she had dreamt of, which would have been impossible had she not met Jack and chosen her own life, instead of the first-class life her parents had chosen for her. The final scene ends with her meeting Jack on Titanic one last time and the other passengers applaud as the two are finally reunited.

STORY #3

"FREE HUGS CAMPAIGN"

In 2006 there was a gentleman by the name of Juan Mann living in London, England. Mann was a tall, lean guy who wore his long hair pulled into a pony tail, the glasses of an intellectual, and a corduroy blazer. He was what conservative people might call the modern version of a hippy. Others have said he looks a little like a scholarly

Jesus. In 2006 he was a nobody.

After a string of bad luck, his life had fallen apart and he was forced to move back to his hometown of Sydney, Australia. Upon arriving at the airport in Sydney he was met by no one. He had no place to call home, and even if he had had a place to go, he would have had nothing more than his carry-on bag of clothing to fill it with. "I was a tourist in my own hometown," he remembers.

Feeling depressed and hopeless, his attention was captured by the families meeting each other in the Arrivals Terminal with warm, loving hugs. His own loneliness made his heart ache with envy at the idea of being hugged and greeted by a loved one, and although most people would have felt self-pity, he was struck with inspiration.

He created a sign that said "FREE HUGS" on both sides and proceeded to the busiest area of the city to hold it aloft. Strangers passed by as if he was invisible, and for 15 minutes he presented his offer without success. A gift of love without cost was feared and avoided by a socially disconnected public.

Disheartened but not defeated, he was approached by an older woman who professed her own sadness because not only had her dog died that morning, but it was also the anniversary of her only daughter's accidental death. What she needed at that moment, when she felt most alone in the world, was a simple hug. He dropped to one knee and they embraced, bonding in mutual sorrow. Both began to smile, despite their circumstances. Neither could have realized the impact that single moment of love between strangers was about to have.

Witnessing this hug, other people began to take Mann up on his offer and accept hugs with surprisingly genuine and heartfelt sincerity. As momentum gained, Mann offered a second poster to strangers and they took up the cause. Soon strangers were hugging each other in groups and adding theatrical elements to increase the fun and spectacle of the whole thing. It truly was a demonstration of – as Mann puts it – "the spirit of humanity."

As the Free Hugs Campaign reached critical mass, public officials became worried about liability and quickly imposed a ban. Juan Mann and his disciples were no longer allowed to hoist their signs, show love to strangers, or congregate in masses of hugging people. Hugging had become illegal.

Outraged at the robotic and heartless ban, the participants in the Free Hugs Campaign began a petition, and as it circulated the media and press got involved, spreading the word to the city of Sydney. After 10,000 people had signed the petition (and hugged the petitioners as thanks) the ban was lifted and the campaign was allowed to flourish.

And flourish it has.

As of the writing of this book, this campaign has been repeated in countries around the planet. In a time when it may feel as if people are becoming less connected and less loving than ever before, the Free Hugs Campaign is a testament to the goodness of people everywhere.

It isn't difficult to understand people being persuaded in these stories, but what do these three stories have in common? In fact they have almost everything in common; it just might be a little hard to see at first. These three persuasive scenarios actually follow precisely the same sequence of events, which we will learn next, in Chapter 0: The 8 Universal Steps of Persuasion.

Chapter 0

The 8 Universal Steps of Persuasion.

ALL PERSUASIONS FOLLOW A BASIC 8-STEP FORMULA.

IF THEY DON'T, THEY FAIL.

Throughout the research for this book, a lot of different types of persuasion were analyzed.

From pop culture elements like music, film, and television, to formal elements like logic and rhetoric. From academic disciplines like psychology and economics to completely non-academic disciplines like seduction and fortune-telling.

The astounding revelation that came from that research was that all of these disciplines follow exactly the same steps, every single time. When the steps are not followed, the persuasions are likely to fail.

Many of the disciplines included in the research were valuable not for their completeness of the 8 Universal Steps, but for their perfection or prowess within a single step. Rhetoric, for example, is the art of presenting a convincing argument, but if the audience already thinks the persuader is a liar, rhetoric alone may not be enough.

Other disciplines were examined because they include most or all of the steps and are very persuasive overall. Psychopolitical brainwashing like the Communism of the 1950's (or now, for that matter) was essentially mass-produced persuasion taken to an extreme. Duplicating those methods on a date or during a job interview, however, is likely to be somewhat counter-productive.

By combining the best of the specialist disciplines into the method of the generalist disciplines, we get a hypothetical persuasion that is the best of everything: The 8 Universal Steps of Persuasion. And they are "steps", not just principles, and are to be followed in order.

CHAPTER 0

THE 8 UNIVERSAL STEPS OF PERSUASION

All persuasion, manipulation, and brainwashing is achieved using the same eight steps, every time.

Before the face-to-face persuasion begins there are two big ideas a persuader must understand:

Step 1. CREATE A GOOD REPUTATION

Step 2. PREDICT YOUR AUDIENCE

During the persuasion there are 5 big things a persuader must accomplish:

Step 3. OPEN & DISARM

Step 4. RAPPORT & NEEDS

Step 5. ISOLATE

Step 6. CONVINCE

Step 7. CLOSE

After the face-to-face persuation, there is one big thing that a persuader must do:

Step 8. SUMMARIZE WITH BIAS

Most people do some of these things intuitively. Without conscious awareness though, steps are usually skipped or performed in the wrong order. All steps will probably seem familiar somehow, but many are actually counter-intuitive.

WHAT ABOUT THAT OTHER METHOD?

There are many, many, quick-and-dirty formulas for communicating and decision-making in the world. If you have to persuade in some way for a living, you probably even use one or two.

In marketing you might use **SIVA** – Solution, Information, Value, Access – or the **Four P's** – Product, Promotion, Price, Place – which are essentially the same thing.

In advertising you might use **another Four P's** – Promise, Picture, Proof, Push. Or the famous copywriting formulas **AIDA(S)** – Attention, Interest, Desire, Action (Satisfaction) or **QUES(T)** – Qualify, Understand, Educate, Stimulate (Transition).

Speeches are typically a joke, introduction, body and conclusion. Sales pitches might be a greeting, qualifier, presentation and close. And rhetorical arguments are typically a thesis, introduction, argument, conclusion and perhaps some discussion.

Even scientific papers are an abstract, introduction, method, results and discussion. However, results often come before methods in more modern journals. That change agrees more with The Composite Persuasion than the traditional format (it's changing for a reason!).

When looking at a list of these formulas, you immediately start to see many common themes. You may also notice that they are quite oversimplified. What is included in an "argument" or "presentation", and what is "interest" or "desire"?

In more formal circles like economics or management theory, it is common to discuss "decision-making models". They are not nearly as complicated as they sound, and basically just try to identify the steps people use to decide... anything. The common problem with all of those models is that they assume people are rational, which we aren't, and that we don't have emotional biases, which we do.

Examples of this approach could be as simple as making a list of pros and cons, or more in-depth, such as: establish objectives, prioritize, identify alternatives, evaluate alternatives, and so on. That might be how a computer would make decisions, but we're not persuading computers.

So how is this book any better?

The Composite Persuasion is a real process based on real persuasions, and the quick-and-dirty formulas helped build it. However, it also upgrades those formulas, because this book includes so many other disciplines as well.

A unifying theory of persuasion, if you will.

The Composite Persuasion is not a simplified abbreviation of one industry's techniques; it fits all persuasions in any industry. It is also not a rational model of decisions, because humans don't always make rational decisions. All decisions, rational or not, can be understood with this method.

It is concrete instead of vague, and not only allows you to predict how people will react to your presentation, but also to analyze your failures and improve next time.

If you have a method that you like, keep using it! Just add The Composite Persuasion to your bag of tricks and create a more well-rounded persuasion. It can be used to *improve* a formula, like the scientific article format, or *complete* a formula, like AIDA(S) or the Four P's.

There is no reason to unlearn what you know. After reading this book you will merely have a better context and method in which to use the knowledge and experience you already have.

THE STORIES, DISSECTED

The stories from the Introduction were chosen to illustrate just how varied the process of persuasion can be while following the 8 steps. In this chapter we will dissect those stories to understand exactly how the 8 Universal Steps of Persuasion work, regardless of context.

Story #1 is fictional and written for this book, but built from real-

BEFORE
ALL ELSE,
BE ARMED.

NICCOLO MACHIAVELLI
ITALIAN DIPLOMAT & AUTHOR

---

life examples of military training. The bed-up-the-hill element was actually more severe in a real account from a former South African soldier. Military recruiting is a form of persuasion that can be argued in several different directions. If you are the enemy, military training is brainwashing. If they are protecting you then they are brave, noble soldiers. If it is your child that is killed in combat, your opinions may start to shift toward manipulation rather than persuasion.

I once saw a graphic of the Grim Reaper with the caption "I support all the troops." Heavy stuff.

Regardless of their perceived position, military recruiting and training practices are highly effective, powerfully long-lasting persuasion techniques.

Story #2 was obviously the basic plot from the movie entitled "Titanic". Released in 1997, it was the highest-grossing box office film of all time, and remains #2 on the list more than a decade later. Titanic beat Lord of The Rings, The Matrix, Star Wars, Harry Potter, and most of the other massively successful movie franchises which also follow the 8 Universal Steps of Persuasion perfectly.

Avatar, which is the #1 movie of all time (also directed by James Cameron), perfectly follows the 8 Steps as well but its fantastic sci-fi elements made it too complicated to use as an example.

In addition to Titanic following the standard blockbuster movie format, the romance/seduction itself also follows the 8 Universal Steps. The ultimate success of this movie may have been the combination of the perfectly-executed movie format with a perfectly-executed love story (just like Avatar), both using the 8 Universal Steps to create irresistibility. A persuasion within a persuasion, if you will.

Story #3 is completely true. The Free Hugs Campaign eventually spanned the entire globe as other people made their own "FREE HUGS" signs and duplicated the effort in cities around the world. The video of the original campaign was voted YouTube's *Video of the Year* in 2006 and has been viewed over 70 million times as of this publication. Juan Mann has appeared on Oprah to further spread the word and even created a charity called Free Help Campaign, to bring help to those truly in need.

Both the real-life campaign and the YouTube video itself were nearly flawless versions of the 8 Universal Steps. If Juan Mann had actually had the same sort of intentions as Jesus during the creation of Christianity, Mann might be one of the more exciting religious leaders in the world right now. Luckily, he just wanted to feel loved.

Many examples of persuasion occur in a scenario where one or more Universal Steps are built-in or unavoidable, and are therefore harder to notice without comparing to the sequence as a whole. Falling in love, eating at a restaurant, or enjoying a catchy song are not exactly "analytical" times in our lives. Once the comparison has been made, however, the steps begin to shine through.

Using the three stories from the introduction we will now get familiar with each step and compare the ways that very different situations can be built from the same ingredients to create effective persuasion. The rest of the book will then dedicate a chapter to each step in detail.

STEP 1: CREATE A GOOD REPUTATION

Every persuasion actually begins before any face-to-face interaction begins. This is the preparation for a first impression. The persuader must understand the way value works – especially social value – and use that to create leadership that others will follow and believe, willingly.

In Story #1 John has lived a life of substandard support and resources. He is an underachiever and is told that regularly. His motivation has been discouraged by others, and his lifestyle has set the stage for John to be persuaded that the misery he lives every day is not what he deserves. Given his situation, who wouldn't want to believe they were worth more?

When the army (the persuader) arrived at John's school to encourage students to attend the military academy they did not dress in normal clothing, or try to be like the students. Students interested in joining the army want to be anything but what they are now. The goal of the persuasion was to convince people like John to become something better, so the soldiers had to become the proof; the credibility; the good reputation. When presenting their case they could not be the awkward, insecure students they once were. They had to be confident, secure soldiers, otherwise they wouldn't be very convincing.

Story #2 is a movie and we are the audience. The movie studio is the persuader. The demonstration of valuable behaviour is not from the characters or the story, but of the movie itself. Is it good? Am I interested? What is it about?

During any movie, as the audience, we have still not decided whether the movie is worth watching until we have watched a significant portion of the film.

A movie's first impression is often created by the trailers released months (and occasionally years) ahead of the actual film. A variety of marketing and advertising efforts, contests, and other anticipation-building devices are employed to create a basic understanding of the movie and the date when it will arrive. Trailers are presented as "teasers" because the less we know, the more we talk and try to figure things out. People will even complain when a trailer gives away too much of the plot, ruining the experience of the film. All of this is built to demonstrate value.

When the time comes to watch the movie in theatres, free passes are given out to the people most likely to be avid fans or press representatives who can spread the good word. At the theatre itself, ideally the line-ups will be out-the-door for the premier; the room will be packed and dark; the audio/visual equipment will provide an experience beyond what can be produced at home. If the preparation for the release and the movie-viewing environment has been executed properly, there will be anticipation in the air.

More people who feel anticipation increases the anticipation of each other person. The movie studios have not given large scenes to pique your interest, they have given little tastes. They assume you will see the movie, rather than asking you politely to please attend if it is convenient. Every movie is the "best... of the year" or some similar statement, even if it is the first movie of the year, of any kind. We are not given the option to decide whether the movie is fantastic or not until we are sitting in the theatre, and by that time the movie studio has succeeded.

But we can also look at Story #2 as a seduction by Jack, since he has successfully and believably persuaded Rose to fall in love with him. His preparation from a life of hard knocks may have taught him that rushing in and asking for what you want is often a bad strategy. Instead he played it cool, maintained his laid-back swagger, and took the time to read and assess Rose and her life. He let his talents speak for themselves, and was patient while she realized his value. Considering the clash of social classes depicted in the movie, this would be an especially contagious boldness in real life. Everyone knows someone who is so "cool", even as a fictional character, that it persuades us to be like them or even adopt their cool behaviour and sayings. The elusive "cool-factor" found in many Hollywood characters is no accident, nor is it elusive.

In Story #3 Juan Mann's life had led him down a path with no rewards. If he had been a content person he may not have been in a position to realize that all people need love and that most people don't get enough. Mann's personality was such that he saw the love of others as something he could achieve and not something wrong with him. Even though it was true that he lacked love at that moment, he was aware that the circumstances of the present have nothing to do with the circumstances of the future, and he took matters into his own hands.

By presenting himself publicly with his "FREE HUGS" sign, he opened the door for anyone and everyone. He didn't sit in a corner and hope for the best, he went out and claimed it. With strangers, our value might only be based on the seconds or minutes they have been aware of us, and Juan Mann made that time count!

The only thing that all of our interactions have in common is us. Therefore it is absolutely necessary that we are "tuned to the right frequency" so people intuitively think we are not just harmless, but socially valuable. This is the art of the first impression. That first impression has very little to do with money, class, physical appearance, or (sadly) truth, even though most people will swear that these things are barriers.

Humans have universal, built-in ingredients that we look for when we meet anyone new and those criteria are almost purely social and behavioural. Those ingredients cause us to see a new person as a potential friend, rather than a potential threat or enemy. Even if they are a potential threat or enemy.

In the next chapter, *Step 1: Create a Good Reputation*, we will look at the details of how and why social value is important and why it works. We will also look at the specific ways that valuable people behave.

STEP 2: PREDICT YOUR AUDIENCE

Every person does quick profiles of other people. On the subway, in the doctor's office, standing in line. All day, every day. How often have you said "she looks like a bitch" or "he thinks he is so great" or "that girl is really cool"?

Anyone who says they don't judge people is lying, and you should take note of the deception. We judge everyone, all the time. We often choose not to discuss those judgements, and the world seems friendlier because of it, but we still do it.

The more pertinent question is: what are we basing those judgements on? Stereotypes? Past experiences? Intuition? All of those are common and unreliable answers. Women in particular are genetically gifted with more tools to assess the emotional character of others. "Women's intuition" includes more parts of the brain dedicated to social skills & communication skills. These mental tools are the reason women are more socially perceptive, more difficult to manipulate, and will burn at the stake while remaining convinced their intuition is perfect. Denial is a powerful thing.

In Story #1 the officers at John's school had it easy. They merely set up a booth, played the part and people with the right profile came to them. But this is no mistake. The recruiters for the Army and other military organizations know very well that their success lies with misbehaved, outcast, and insecure people: those who want to belong to something. People who have had a hard life and little social success are the perfect candidates for a tightly regimented, brotherhood-style system of discipline. A typical, spoiled upper class genius may be what the Army would like to have in some cases, but the idea of strict, mindless obedience is the opposite of what turns them on. A different type of persuasion would be needed; perhaps one aimed at their lack of physical confidence, and need for intellectual dominance. If you've ever wondered how spies are recruited, this is a good start.

In Story #2, just as in all movies, the writers must take advantage of our natural interest in things like profit and loss, good and evil, love and sex, and so on, which we cover in *Step 2: Predict Your Audience*. The story of Titanic is an epic one, of death and survival, and the movie pairs that storyline with romantic seduction and true love. We are even teased with a nude portrait at the beginng, and we know it must be drawn at some point in the movie.

In the seduction part of Titanic, Jack observes Rose and sees that she does not enjoy the life of luxury. She admits in the movie that Jack "sees people." She feels trapped in her engagement, and envious of Jack's freedom. Throughout the movie he maintains these characteristics, even when having dinner with Rose's family. He is resilient and confident. He then takes Rose to the 3rd Class party – a "real" party – and shows her what she's missing. Without being able to read her and know what she liked and needed, he would have failed. If he had tried to become like her fiancé to win her, he also would have failed. People can only protect what they have, and can only want what they don't. Offering someone what they already have is not persuasive unless they will benefit from having more of it.

In Story #3 Juan Mann's understanding of people's need for love came from his own circumstances. He felt a need and therefore immediately recognized it in others. In order to find the people who lacked love he created a sign and went to the busiest place available. He played a numbers game and won. In this book we will never rely on chance for success, but in Mann's case, the odds were in his favour.

Excellent human behaviour knowledge comes to us from the disciplines that benefit most from being able to predict how a person will act, before they choose to act that way: fortune-tellers, criminal profilers, psychologists, spies, demographers, marketers, and pick-up artists. These disciplines, among others, understand a great deal about human behaviour and can perform their services because of it.

Fortune tellers use "cold reading" techniques to tell a person they have never met about that person's life and personality and relationships, all with relative accuracy. Criminal profilers can tell what type of person is committing crimes based on the way in which the crimes are committed. Demographers and marketers can create "personas" of the types of people using products and services to make targeted advertising. Pick-Up Artists profile desirable women and use their understanding of seduction to custom-build a persuasion that creates sexual attraction.

Understanding the other person begins before the interaction and continually improves throughout our experience with that person. We will start with a general understanding and let it grow into a tailored approach as we learn about them. Eventually you will be able to communicate exactly the way they want you to.

Mastery of human motivations will give you a distinct advantage in any communication, and a seemingly psychic intuition when it comes to persuasion. It also allows you to understand yourself and the irrational things you do every day (whether you admit it or not).

STEP 3: OPEN & DISARM

Beginning an interaction with a stranger can be very intimidating for many people. We are all taught as children not to talk to strangers, even though only 1% of child abductions are committed by strangers. It is a powerful example of an instinctual fear.

When we begin an interaction with another person, the first and foremost goal is merely to get the conversation in motion and disarm their assumptions or fears.

In Story #1 John's introduction to the army was one of promises. The very first statement from the Army officer to John was "the Army wants you to be all you can be." No one else had ever said that, and in terms of self-interest, it's a winner. The subsequent explanations of being paid and being important would only have amplified the effect.

In Story #2 the movie itself used a subtle but clever approach to engage our interest from the beginning. Most people are familiar with the story of Titanic, and knew the movie was essentially a love story, so when the first scene takes place with some scientists underwater the audience experiences a moment of "what is going on?" Curiosity is hard to resist.

When we meet Jack for the first time it is during a tense moment in a game of poker and all players are about to show their hands for a big pot. We are immediately engaged. As far as the persuasion of the movie is concerned, Step 3 is a big success.

During Jack's seduction of Rose, a conversation takes place when

Rose is standing on the edge of the rail contemplating suicide. While the normal first reaction might be to care for her safety, Jack takes the opposite approach and cunningly makes her aware of the icy cold water by talking about how when he dives in after her, he will not enjoy it. Given the circumstances, this approach definitely gets Rose's attention.

In Story #3 Juan Mann certainly has one of the best conversation starters. "FREE HUGS" is a disarmingly simple and selfless offer, and it almost breaks your heart to watch people noticing and resisting his offer during the initial seconds of the video. The crowd is thinking "is this guy crazy?" and "Is he going to rob me during the hug?"

It is only once the old lady accepts (after starting a conversation) and disarms the concerns of everyone else that Mann succeeds.

Pick-up artists aptly call this step "opening" because it opens the person to further persuasion.

When the police initially "open & disarm" a criminal, they introduce themselves and literally take away his weapons. Now that the criminal has been disarmed it is safe to move in for, shall we say, more intimate conversation.

Interestingly, what a persuader says during the opening (assuming it is done confidently) has no effect on the overall outcome and doesn't even have to be remotely true to effectively open a conversation.

We will discuss methods to initiate a conversation and remove skepticism in detail in the chapter entitled *Step 3: Open & Disarm*.

STEP 4: CREATE RAPPORT & NEEDS

In any persuasion the persuader must use the needs of the other person as leverage to get what they want. The classic example is a trade; you do something for me and I will do something for you. But not all persuasion requires sacrifice, and the best persuasion merely requires an understanding of human nature.

The more desperately a person feels a need for something, the more suggestible they become. They may even use the word "need" for something they just "want".

Simultaneously the persuader must build trust (or believability) and friendship. A trusting, friendly feeling between two people is called "rapport".

In Story #1 the recruiting officers, the people in the Army registration office, and even the General on the first day of boot camp all present a friendly, serious, accepting environment that appears dedicated and supportive of John's success. His parents do not support the idea, which ultimately creates even more emotional distance. John's need is to feel important, to escape the shackles of his town, his family, and everyone's low expectations, and realize the potential he has always seen in himself. The friendly and honourable Army seems eager to do that for him. Once John accepts, however, he realizes just what he has got himself into.

In Story #2, we as the audience need to relate to the main characters and feel sympathy or hope for their situation. We are being persuaded to become engaged in the movie's story, so the writers make us like certain characters, and hate others. As much as it may feel like we choose the characters we like, everyone chooses the same characters, and that isn't a coincidence. By introducing us to the characters and highlighting their good and bad traits we immediately relate to the "good guys".

Good guys like Jack and Rose are down-to-earth, confident, and friendly. We immediately fall for them. "Bad guys" like Rose's family are emotionless, condescending, and have little in common with most people. Adding the "Rich vs. Poor" aspect of the movie only helps the cause, since only a small minority of the audience are rich, and we hate them for it when they think they are better than us "commoners".

We love to hate the bad guys.

When the good guys are presented with a challenge we want them to succeed, especially when the odds are against them. Their needs become our needs. For the bad guys on the other hand, we "hope" for them to die, be hurt, be destroyed, to lose, or any other ill fate the screenwriter employs. Bad guys are no longer people, they are the enemy, just like in war.

During Jack's seduction of Rose, Jack quickly identifies her need to feel free and to be loved (two things all people need) rather than controlled (which nobody likes). He demonstrates all the freedom and optimism in his life and she falls in love with the idea of his life and subsequently, him.

In Story #3 most people's need was to be loved. Society is not always as welcoming to a vulnerable or unloved person as we would like when we have that need. By making his "FREE HUGS" sign and holding it up in public he actually acknowledged a need and became the solution all in one motion. It is situations like this, in which steps become invisible or covert, when it is often difficult to see the 8 Universal Steps of Persuasion.

For persuasion to exist we must have a need. Since the other person doesn't live to satisfy our needs the persuader must create or recognize the other person's needs. Whether they actually "need" something or merely desire it, is irrelevant.

"Identifying a need" as leverage is a concept that can seem immoral at first, but is done intuitively by most people. Have you ever questioned a restaurant for taking advantage of your need for food? What about being furious at stores for making you pay for a drink when you're thirsty? Probably not.

If we put a gun to someone's head, they fear for their lives and will be very easily persuaded to do even the most ludicrous things. They "need" to stay alive. Motivating a person and creating a need, like all aspects of persuasion, is only as immoral as you make it.

We will be learning about much more subtle methods than a gun-

MEN FREELY BELIEVE THAT WHICH THEY DESIRE.

GAIUS JULIUS CAESAR
ROMAN EMPEROR

to-the-head approach, but the objective is the same: create a need that must be solved.

When the army officers first met John they were friendly, confident, accepting, and seemed motivated to help him achieve his goals. John obviously liked that, so they created rapport quickly.

In Titanic we begin to like Jack and Rose because we see qualities in them that we see in ourselves (whether we actually have those traits or not). Once we are in their pocket, the movie leads us through an emotional rollercoaster.

Juan Mann wagered that other people had the same need as him (which all people do). Once people began to relate to him and accept his Free Hugs he was able to recruit other people to "pass it on", and he became the leader of a movement.

Rapport creates a sense of trust, bonding, common goals, and friendship, even when the persuader has just met the other person, and it goes both ways. Although rapport may be created on purpose, it can result in genuine feelings of friendship for the persuader too. Rapport can also be resisted to create attraction and "charm", based on the same principles.

The persuader will then use the friendship they have created to demonstrate that they are the means to an end. To do this, the persuader will make the other person work for approval and to satisfy whatever motivation has been ignited.

In Story #1 the Army wants to make John "all he can be". Without them he will be where he is already, approaching life failure. All he has to do is enlist.

In Story #2 the movie (like all Hollywood movies) gives the main characters a need. If the need was impossible to solve, the movie would be terrible. What would the characters do for the last hour if they weren't trying to be with each other? There would be no story.

In Titanic, the boat itself is merely the setting for a love story, and the iceberg and the sinking of the ship are merely tools to create excitement and emotion. If that seems superficial, keep in mind that this movie has earned about 25 cents for every person on the planet.

During Jack's seduction of Rose she needs only to be with him to receive everything she wants. Rose can't get Jack's benefits (so to speak) from her fiancé, so she must choose Jack or live without.

In Story #3 Juan Mann is holding a sign that says FREE HUGS. Any one of those people could have hugged any other person near them, but he was the only one offering, so he became the solution.

The secret to Step 4 is when the persuader uses a need and rapport to make the other person "qualify" to be persuaded. It is easily the most elegant and counter-intuitive element in persuasion, but is incredibly effective when done well.

We will discuss exactly how this works in *Step 4: Create Rapport & Needs*.

STEP 5: ISOLATE

It is very important in any persuasion to have a clear and uninterrupted channel for communication. Everyone loses when there are distractions or competing persuaders. The person being persuaded will find it difficult to make any choice at all.

In Story #1 John is brought to boot camp for his training. He is cut off from the outside world and only allowed to do, be, or think what the Army allows.

In Story #2 isolation is built in. In a movie theatre we are placed in total darkness and the sound is loud enough to drown out everything around us. We even forget about the people around us for much of the experience. However, isolation is also a common weakness with a movie. If we are watching a movie at home during distractions or preoccupations, we will often feel it wasn't a good film.

Jack's efforts to win Rose almost fail in the movie because of the pressure from her family. When she buckles and tells him she can't be with him anymore, he takes her to a private part of the ship and gets serious with her, performing a masterful job of making himself the solution. It is after this that they truly begin to fall in love.

In Story #3 the hugging element becomes an excellent form of figurative isolation. During and after a hug there is such a strong momentary bond between two people that Mann was able to talk other people into helping him with his cause.

We will look at the three forms of isolation and how they are used, in *Step 5: Isolate*.

STEP 6: CONVINCE

Convincing someone implies that there is some resistance. In many situations the persuasive power of the earlier steps may be enough that the persuasion has already been successful. In other situations, especially when persuasion happens over a longer period of time, there will be a significant element of convincing.

This step requires that information is presented in small steps toward the larger, final agreement, in a way that is easy to understand and never boring.

In Story #1 John's training is the convincing step. He is given precisely the same schedule all day, every day, and the task of pushing his bed up the hill, which seems insurmountable, but he eventually succeeds. His training lasts for years, progressively involving more and more committment, including the instruction of others.

In Story #2 the Hollywood movie structure is built so that after we have accepted the characters and their goal, we will watch them go through a series of tests or events that build on one another as the story progresses. This is the way every good story is built, whether it is on film or not. Just when we can predict the plot, Jack and Rose make love. Later when their escape from the sinking ship seems obvious, Jack suddenly faces the challenge of being hancuffed to the pipe. This maintains our interest, even in the predictable parts.

In Jack's seduction of Rose they venture into a series of encounters, each more sensual and sexually charged than the last, including the infamous nude drawing scene.

In Story #3 the Free Hugs Campaign nearly came to a standstill after a few people had been convinced and it became a small phenomenon. When the police banned the Campaign it was given the resistance it needed to gain larger scale attention and a reason to convince people on a larger scale. Using the press and the petition, the Free Hugs Campaign changed from a small spectacle into a movement, one signature at a time.

Juan Mann convinced one person at a time, then multiple people at a time, and eventually millions of people at a time to build his Campaign.

If he had just sent 70 million emails from the start he surely would have failed.

We will learn about the major patterns of convincing someone to agree in *Step 6: Convince,* which also includes Tips & Tricks collected from every persuasive communication style within the scope of this book.

STEP 7: CLOSE

On the internet we call the close a "call-to-action". You might know it as the "Buy" button.

Closing is often described as the most mysterious and challenging part of persuasion. If the other Universal Steps have been performed well, the close should be effortless. At the very least it should look effortless. Any good close includes the means to immediately commit, even if it seems unnecessary. For example, when asking someone to give you their number, have your phone ready or give them a pen.

Otherwise a little confidence and assumptive delivery go a long way.

In Story #1 the close is when John is sent to war. His training and the construction of his attitudes towards himself, his country, and war culminate in his execution of orders during combat. You could also see it as a type of close when he enlists in the first place, from the point of view of the recruiter.

In Story #2 the movie's close is when the main characters succeed or fail. When it becomes clear that they are at the do-or-die moment our suspense is at its maximum. Sometimes a movie will use an "empty close" that makes it appear that the characters have failed, only to reveal that they have actually succeeded beyond expectations. In Titanic, the Love Story close happens when Jack and Rose make love in the car. Pick-up artists would call that an "F-Close".

In Story #3 Juan Mann's individual persuasions are quick, so the actual hug becomes a close. It is a close when he gets other people to hold the sign as well, and when he succeeds in getting petition signatures. When someone else agrees to our goal, that is a close. If we require a series of small closes to achieve a much larger goal, then each "yes" we get is a milestone on that path.

The YouTube video for the Free Hugs Campaign not only follows the 8 Universal Steps fairly well, but is accompanied by a song that matches. The video positions the success of the petition as the close element, and it is quite emotional to watch.

STEP 8: SUMMARIZE WITH BIAS

After the persuasive interaction ends there is one more important step to complete, and that is to ensure that the persuasion is remembered positively. Any good persuasion leaves the persuaded person feeling good about their choices. And in the event that the persuasion really wasn't very positive, we need to make some adjustments to that memory before they leave.

In Story #1 John is presented with numerous awards and remembered as a hero, even though his military career has included killing and destruction. John has also been responsible for training and promoting other soldiers the way he was, which ensures that the values instilled in him will be passed on to future generations, and that he feels pride for his accomplishments.

In Story #2, like in most movies, a happy ending is the best way to get universal acceptance. The writers of Titanic were writing about a tragic disaster, and Jack dies in the icy waters before Rose is saved. If they ended the movie there, it would feel very unsatisfying.

As the movie concludes, they reveal that Rose's life was forever changed (some would say it was saved) by Jack and she achieved everything she wanted because of him. The last moment shows Rose and Jack being reunited in the afterlife to unanimous applause from the rest of the passengers. In the seduction of Jack, we are left to assume that Rose feels good about it, since the entire movie was her recollection of those events.

So after hundreds of people die, including the main character, we are left with good feelings. Brilliant!

In Story #3 Juan Mann has become an icon and the Free Hugs Campaign has gone around the globe, including a new charity built by the same people. Nobody seems to wonder what happened to Juan Mann to cause such a crash in his life, or why there was no one at the airport to meet him that day. Indeed, it would be quite cynical to even ask.

As the interaction ends we will also want to make the final

moments as positive as possible. We will learn about several clever ways to do this in *Step 8: Summarize with Bias.*

Hopefully throughout this chapter you have become somewhat more familiar with the fundamental, universal steps of persuasion. Throughout the rest of the book you will learn each step in detail with a lot of examples and skills you can apply to your own persuasions.

All steps exist in all effective persuasions, all the time. No case is unique or impossible. The personality or special interests of the person you are persuading only changes minor details of a persuasion, not the method. As you read this book you will also learn to recognize the steps as they happen to you, so you can avoid manipulation. You will begin to see people's actions for what they are. Next you will learn to be valuable in *Step 1: Create A Good Reputation.*

STEP
01

Create A Good Reputation

Build value through behavior & environment.

YOUR
PARENTS WERE
WRONG.

I am about to disagree with something millions of parents have said to millions of children: You <u>should</u> care about what other people think of you.

A lot.

Undoubtedly, if your parents ever told you to ignore the opinions of other people it was because those opinions were negative. Presumably your parents selectively changed their philosophy when everyone was impressed with you. Suddenly everyone's opinion of you was spot-on. How convenient.

By ignoring or avoiding the opinions of everyone else we are ignoring something that is potentially very powerful when it comes to persuasion: your reputation. By learning how a reputation is built and by learning where your weaknesses may be, you can influence what other people think of you. It might have been easier to swallow the idea that everyone else just didn't see the real (and fantastic!) you, but you might be happier with the results if you change your approach instead.

Like with many problems, ignoring it doesn't actually make it go away. So not only should you care about what other people think of you, you should control it too.

Good persuaders hold this to be self-evident.

WHAT IS REPUTATION?

A reputation is a slippery concept. All the impressions we make on a person add up to be our credibility, respectability, and trustworthiness; our reputation. A reputation is how a person would describe you to a stranger, when you're not listening.

A reputation is equally – or sometimes more – important when a person has never met us before. In a situation with a stranger, they will make major decisions about us based on whatever they experience of us during that first encounter. While your old friends may overlook a few bad experiences because they have had so many good ones, a stranger will not.

This may seem intimidating at first, and probably contributes to the anxiety of meeting new people. Fortunately, the information they have, like how honest or confident or likable we are, is completely under our control.

Reputation played a significant role in most disciplines included in this book. In every movie we are always introduced to the characters in such a way that we are aware of their past, their values, and their position in life so we can assess their reputation and how we should think about that character. Journalists will "angle" a story in a certain way so that the subject will seem like a good, brave, evil, elusive, impressive, or normal person so that our sympathies will shift in a certain direction (e.g. – "Family man loses everything in fire"). Public relations experts spend most of their time managing the reputations of people, companies, and their products and services.

Investment advice coming from a person living on the street will probably fall on deaf ears, even if he legitimately has good information to offer. A person who is caught telling lies is branded a "liar" and the validity of everything they say in the future seems more questionable.

On the other hand, a good reputation can give you a halo, even when you don't deserve it. Someone who lives in a big house with a fancy car might be asked for investment advice, even when they are clueless. The person living on the street could be a former Wall Street broker, while the rich person could be a housewife on a farm. Then again, would you trust a failed broker over a housewife that has been so successful? Reputation is perception, and only perception.

A good reputation is built by using behavior and a supporting environment to create two things: value and trust.

Value (Confidence)

A person that understands what makes them valuable will act with confidence because they realize their value. Over a long period of time this valuable and confident behavior will have benefits beyond measure.

Trust (Believability)

Good reputations almost always necessitate that a person can be trusted. Whether you are being trusted with responsibility, trusted to tell the truth (or not to say anything), or trusted to deliver good results, if the other person doesn't think you have the right intentions, any persuasion will be an uphill battle.

Being believable is similar to trust, but even if you are trusted, you may have to demonstrate your ability to follow through on promises or competences before someone will believe that you are someone to whom they should listen. The more you will gain from a suggestion you make for someone else, the more your believability may be drawn into question.

I tend to trust skydiving more than bungee jumping, because if my skydiving instructor makes a mistake, he will be strapped to my back. If the bungee jumping company makes a mistake, they get bad PR and higher insurance premiums. My evaluation of risk may be misguided, but you must admit, one of those seems more comforting than the other.

In most cases, trust and believability go hand in hand.

WHY IS REPUTATION IMPORTANT?

Without a good reputation every persuasion is over before it begins, which is why it is Step 1. If you have a bad reputation with the person being persuaded, your first goal is to fix it. If you have no reputation, that's good! It's time to start making a good one. Without a good reputation nothing a persuader says will have any value. And value is exactly what this step is all about.

Reputation provides context. The human world is built on social rules, situations, and expectations. During our lives we will experience people from all parts of the social spectrum, from prostitutes to millionaires, and we associate certain things with certain types of people. Whether we like to admit it or not, we want to be near people (and be the people) at the high end of the spectrum, and we try to avoid those at the lower end of the spectrum. We should no longer blindly follow that instinct.

We are more likely to lend a dollar to a casual friend than to a dirty, homeless man, as sad as that may seem. Would you be surprised if your friend didn't give money to the homeless man, because he assumes it would be used to buy alcohol? Would you be more surprised if your friend lent you a dollar for a snack, moments later? Who really needed that money? Who did your friend trust instead? This is reputation in action. Your reputation was good, and the homeless man's was, shall we say, less so.

Let's look at a different situation: imagine a persuader is trying to impress someone they like or someone powerful. Many people's first instinct when trying to impress is to be as helpful as possible, or to jump at every opportunity to cater to the person they are trying to persuade. It seems logical; they might notice and appreciate us if we're always there to lend a hand, right?

Nope.

People who take this approach become a "yes man" or a "brown noser" or what some people might call a "follower" (not the good Twitter kind). A follower inherently has less value than a leader. There are more of them, they are replaceable, and nobody asked them to be there. There is nothing that will make you less persuasive than being someone without value, socially speaking.

After explaining this concept I have found that some people are compelled to resist. For many, the compulsion to be useful when they want to impress people is so automatic that it may seem difficult to imagine another possibility. There is nothing wrong with helping people, but the way persuaders help people makes a difference.

Through learning about so many persuasive disciplines, I have come to believe that the *Helpfulness Problem* lies in one common logical flaw: people often associate being useful with being important. Far too many people will work overtime because they can't say no to unreasonable requests. Or stay in a horrible relationship because the other person "needs you and can't live without you."

The idea that "trying harder" will make you more likable, more lovable, or more valuable is, in essence, the same problem. I have watched people try to catch and hold a cat that is afraid of them to make the cat not be afraid anymore. Not surprisingly, they get the opposite result. Their strategy is "more of the same" instead of trying something different. According to Einstein, that makes them insane.

Whether a follower is trying to be useful, forcing themselves on someone, apologizing constantly, being silent while someone takes what they want, or anything similar, the other person has the value and the follower is just trying to get attention (or avoid ridicule).

Value is made, not earned. As soon as someone else has the power to determine your value, you have no value. They can take it away just as easily. If there is one concept to take from this book, the Principle of Value would be a good choice.

The Composite Persuasion does not include begging or hoping or being dependent on someone else. As my good friend Peter once said, "There is a fine line between a doorman and a doormat." If you only do things for other people then you are not valuable, you are useful, and useful people get used.

If you have ever loved someone who didn't love you back then you already know exactly what we're talking about here. You feel helpless and desperate to make them want you, but the harder you try, the worse it gets.

The problem in that situation is your perception of value, and by understanding value you will learn how to become valuable in the eyes of someone else (not to mention yourself).

Value can take different forms. For example, someone who is introduced as an expert is immediately given extra importance. An expert can convince many otherwise intelligent people of outrageous lies, based primarily on the strength of her reputation. A person introduced as a pathological liar may have difficulty convincing anyone of anything, even if they are actually an expert.

The 'boy who cried wolf' may come to mind.

Ultimately a reputation can be created in a matter of seconds or over a lifetime of interactions with another person. A good short reputation is easier, but a good long reputation is more powerful. Both require an understanding of how value works, and how to communicate our value properly. Once we have that understanding, both types of reputation almost build themselves.

THE PRINCIPLE OF VALUE

My favorite example of value is a diamond. A diamond is a rock, and when it comes out of the ground it is not particularly amazing. It's kind of dull actually, looking like quartz or shiny salt. But after the proper care and craftsmanship it becomes a sparkling, expensive, almost magical piece of jewelry. Just like glass, cubic zirconium, or clear plastic could, given the same treatment.

Diamonds are a symbol of status among the rich, and the bigger the better. They are the chosen stones to represent marriage or engagement in many cultures. "Diamonds are a girl's best friend," apparently. Diamonds are so special that they require a trained expert to estimate their value and quality.

PRICE IS WHAT YOU PAY. VALUE IS WHAT YOU GET.

WARREN BUFFET
BILLIONAIRE, BUSINESSMAN

We assume the price of a diamond reflects how valuable it is, and we will spend enough to make sure our engagement ring demonstrates our status. The "two months' salary" rule for a diamond engagement ring was created by the people who sell diamonds. Are you surprised?

Now, consider a situation during which you went into a store, paid two months' salary for a well-cut piece of crystal, in a beautiful setting, and believed it was a diamond. It looked like a diamond, everyone else thought it was diamond, and you never thought to question it. The store clerk, dressed in a smart suit, described its origins and craftsmanship with exquisite detail, and a calm, informed tone. His store had been operating for decades, and his father, like him, had been a dealer of only the finest gems, cut by the finest craftsmen. The only problem is that he sold you a piece of crystal worth nothing compared to the diamond you paid for. Years go by, and you eventually pass away, never realizing that your diamond was actually a crystal.

The question is: does it matter?

Of course, it was fraud, which is immoral and illegal. However, you didn't know that, and experienced all the good feelings, and admiration you would have experienced from a real diamond. All the parties where women fawned over the size and clarity of the diamond, secretly jealous. All the boasting to men who pretended to be knowledgeable about the industry and joked about having a lower salary than you. All exactly the same with the crystal as it would have been with a diamond.

So, does it matter? The answer is that emotionally it might, but practically it doesn't. When you buy a diamond you buy status and satisfaction – and maybe a demonstration of your love – and the diamond is just your chosen method. Some people choose a Ferrari, or a house, or a hug. Some people just elope to Vegas.

We can also look at value from the point of view of the diamond. If you are the diamond – the most valuable rock in the world - you are desired by everyone, but only affordable to a few. Imagine the prestige! Every person that walks into the store sees you and instantly desires you because you are unattainable and special. You may like that they want to buy you, but you're not worried when they can't. You appreciate the value of a pearl or a ruby, but you're definitely not threatened by them. You may even feel sorry for buyers when they are not fortunate enough to have you. You're calm, happy, and confident because with so much value, it is only a matter of time before you are purchased by someone impressive. Once they pay the price, of course.

In addition, diamonds are probably displayed among other diamonds, and not the cheaper jewelry. There is probably a little extra attention paid to the way you and your fellow diamonds look in the store. A bigger display case, more space for each of you, and nicer lighting. Your price may not be displayed at all, because the type of person interested in you wants the best, and money is not a factor. "If you have to ask, you probably can't afford it."

So why have diamonds become so valuable?

Value is created by two factors: how much of something there is, and how many people want it. Economists call this "scarcity and demand". In the case of diamonds, they are hard to acquire – especially the big ones – and a lot of people want them.

But wait – am I saying that people only want things because other people want those things too?

Yes! And the amount of something that is available can be chosen by the supplier! There are even rumors of diamond companies stockpiling diamonds to reduce the number available, which increases the value. Whether or not that is true, it would work.

Robert Cialdini's, *Influence: The Psychology of Persuasion*, was the first book that attempted to describe persuasion, and he brought "Social Proof" into mainstream consciousness. Social Proof is the demonstration that other people want or like something too. What Cialdini failed to emphasize was that scarcity is also necessary to create social value, not merely social proof (he described scarcity as a separate principle). It's about how many people want something, not how many people have it. The more people that own big diamonds, the *less* valuable they become.

If we walk into a store, and we're not a diamond expert, then we will trust anyone who is a diamond expert (or says they are) to tell us what is high quality and valuable. The beautiful and scary thing about value is that it doesn't have to be true that lots of people want something. It just has to be believable.

So how does this apply to persuasion? Should we sell everyone crystals and say their diamonds? Certainly not. We should, instead, learn that it is the emotional value of something that matters, and that value is based on the belief that something is wanted and rare. Luckily for us, there is nothing rarer than a person; there is only one of you.

In persuasion we need our value to be believable, and that is accomplished by creating a valuable environment and behaving like a diamond (if a diamond thought or behaved). Once a persuader begins acting like they're socially valuable, they become valuable. We will put this principle to work in *Step 3: Open & Disarm*. The important part for now is to understand that value is perception, not cost. No matter how much you sacrifice to feel useful, the only real value comes from how valuable you seem. And this is always true.

CREATE VALUE IN YOUR ENVIRONMENT

It is important to realize that while valuable behavior is similar for all people in all cultures, a valuable environment must suit the situation. If you are trying to get donations and your office is in the top floor of a fancy skyscraper, it might be hard to convince someone that you're desperately in need, or using the donations wisely. However, with a moderate office, older computers, and a décor that says "we can't afford this place"... you might be on the right track.

This is the value of value. Understanding the idea of applying value to yourself and your environment will immediately make you more persuasive as a person, and make your persuasions more convincing in general. Here are some of the endless examples of how these concepts are used in the real world:

Real Estate is an industry built on these principles, and almost nothing else. The same house in two different neighborhoods would have two different values. Location, location, location. If one of those houses had been owned by someone famous, more value again. Usually when a house is put on the market there are "showings". Houses are often "staged" as well, meaning a professional designer has furnished the interior in a flattering way. The main purpose of having these showings is to allow potential buyers to see that other people are interested in the property as well, and to experience the emotional value of the house in person.

The agent will give tours of the house (while dressed respectably) highlighting all of the potential of the property in terms of lifestyle, enjoyment, and possibly advantages over the buyer's current home. The original price is based on logic: features versus location. The agent will then manage the bidding process in such a way that every bidder is aware of the other offers. The house suddenly becomes worth more if someone else is willing to pay more. In the end, the most emotional value + enough money = the highest offer.

Fortune Tellers sell a service that has little or no actual value other than emotional satisfaction. Using their expert knowledge of cold reading techniques (linguistic tricks and careful observation) they are able to make it appear that they know things that they don't, so creating a believable perception of value is at the core of their success. This should also be an example to the people who feel that they don't have value. Fortune Telling literally has no practical value – everything they say is either false, or is something you already knew, and you can't actually use any of it– but they have been around for hundreds of years, if not more, and they make a lot of people feel better.

ACTION EXPRESSES PRIORITIES.

MOHONDAS GHANDI
INDIAN IDEOLOGICAL LEADER

The place in which a "reading" will take place is usually carefully constructed to present an image of mystique. Candles, incense, mystical artwork, music, costumes, books, tarot cards, a Ouija board, and anything else to support the idea that an other-worldly event will take place. The fortune tellers themselves are calm, confident, and friendly. They are there to help you find answers, even if you don't know the questions yet. It is a supportive place and they are your guide to... somewhere else. There is never doubt in their minds. If the reading goes poorly, it is your fault for being skeptical, or having bad energy, never their fault. They will ensure that the customer leaves with a feeling of satisfaction and hope for the future; the real service being provided.

Religion, as with many elements of persuasion, is one of the most masterful examples of value. Religions have sometimes had millennia to perfect the way they communicate their value and prepare their environments for maximum persuasion. Church architecture is well-known among architects for its emotional effect. The entry room often has a low ceiling and small proportions – human proportions – to make you feel comfortable, but that is the only room in a church where you are meant to feel comfortable. The main hall has huge dimensions, echoing acoustics, and is covered in larger-than-life artwork, all to make you feel awe. Windows are often placed near the ceiling and only at the front where the priest delivers the sermon, in front of the huge statue of Jesus. Both are bathed in heavenly light, while the audience is left in the shade. Even non-religious people speak in a hushed tone when they enter old European churches, and certain clothing is required - so as not to offend the Lord - which makes each participant a piece of the persuasive environment. After centuries of persuading the masses, the effect of religious reputation is extremely powerful, even before anyone has said a word.

When the time to speak arrives, the best religious leaders are amazingly adept at public speaking and when being interviewed. They maintain a confident, passionate, sympathetic tone throughout, while dodging and manipulating the interviewer or audience past the gaping holes in religious gospel. Politicians have nothing on world religious leaders in terms of being persuasive speakers, and religious leaders know it. Evangelists seem to only feel at home on a stage where they can project their leadership onto masses of loyal followers.

Religious ceremonies are built to give the priest the power to absolve sins, bestow the love of a God, and make followers feel better about themselves. If you know of a better display of value, I'd like to see it.

Interrogators, in contrast, could be seen as the opposite of Fortune Tellers and religious leaders. This is because, for the most part, they deal strictly with the cold, hard truth, as opposed to beautiful, fulfilling fiction. They are focused on real and immediate consequences. But emotion is just as much a weapon for them as it is for a fortune teller.

Interrogations usually take place in a stark room, void of decoration and distraction. The interrogator becomes more powerful because he or she is the only thing in the room other than the criminal. Their value is understood by everyone, and is demonstrated with freedom; something the suspect doesn't have. They ask the questions and the criminal responds, period. No fun, no hope, no warm and fuzzy emotional satisfaction. And it is very effective.

The interrogator will wear a uniform that identifies her as the leader, she will act like the leader, and she, ideally, will never allow the suspect to deviate from the interrogator's leadership. If a "deal" is offered it would only demonstrate further that the interrogator has power to give. And ultimately the interrogator works for the police who have been given power from governments, supported by citizens. Interestingly, sometimes the criminal has information the interrogator needs, and could therefore become a leader (and reverse the persuasion), but the deck is stacked against them.

Pick-Up Artists specialize in seduction. Whether it is in a club, or a café, or while waiting for the light to turn green, displaying value is of the utmost importance, and it has to happen quickly. "Picking up" a woman happens in 4-7 hours (on average) in a club, or in just minutes on the street. The Pick Up Artist (PUA) will approach a woman they have never met and proceed to demonstrate the specific traits that women find most attractive in a man. Confidence, assertiveness, decisiveness, humour, and social value. We will get into the specifics of sexual attraction in *Step 2: Predict Your Audience*, but suffice it to say that displaying value – especially for a man – is most of it. Whether it is the attention-seeking clothing they wear or the extreme comfort they show in the presence of beautiful women, everything about picking up is about value.

The environment for a PUA is a fluid concept, because it consists mostly of other people. They will circulate in a room introducing themselves to everyone, if only to be able to wave at those people later, demonstrating their popularity. When they approach a group of people they will first ignore the person they want and focus on wooing or disarming her friends. This creates an environment of acceptance and fun that is hard to resist. Assuming the woman they want has been paying attention, the PUA's previous circulation around the room has also shown her that the PUA is an important person and the fact that he has chosen her is important.

Online Sales may seem like a far cry from persuasions like religion and interrogation, but the steps are the same. On a website the language and graphic design chosen to represent a brand can have a significant impact on the perception of whether that brand is trustworthy or successful. It has been shown that during the payment process on a website it takes only a few tenths of a second for a person to decide whether the website looks trustworthy. This is the environment for the persuasion to make a purchase.

Websites that are well known like Amazon and Google, can inherently "convert" more people into purchasers than unknown sites, purely based on the strength of their reputation.

Infomercials tend to be rather blunt examples of the 8 Universal Steps of Persuasion. During a 30-minute infomercial several tactics will be used to solidify the credibility and reputation of the product being sold. During the opening seconds we are often introduced to "experts" in a particular area that is relevant to the product, or celebrities that are prepared to give their endorsement. The product itself is new and being introduced for the first time, so it is necessary to rely on the reputation of the endorsers to provide value. The product will then be dramatically demonstrated repeatedly throughout the infomercial, complete with several witnesses acting impressed and excited each time (even if they just saw it 5 minutes ago). The environment is a television studio, and therefore is anything they need it to be, including lighting, make-up, clothing, and realistic (but pre-arranged) "scientific tests". Infomercials sometimes fail in their believability, and instead just look "over-the-top". By trying a little too hard, they lose value and we begin to see through the act.

Animal Training may seem like another unusual example when discussing value in persuasion, but it may actually be the best. Humans, whether we like it or not, are animals. We respond to all the same types of training and conditioning as animals, we just do it at a more sophisticated level. I once watched a reality show where dog trainers taught women their techniques, which then worked like a charm on their husbands. Pick Up Artists learn the same things for use on women in clubs, and they work just as well. Anyone who has ever watched Cesar Millan, The Dog Whisperer, knows the immediate impact that displaying value can have in an interaction, and most of the time he is teaching the owners more than the pets. On nearly every episode Millan demonstrates how a pack animal like a dog or a human will respond to someone who can confidently and calmly take command of a situation.

Politics is a rather obvious example. American presidential candidates, for example, spend months and even years travelling the country, buying advertising, and meeting people face-to-face in order to create a reputation that the majority of Americans consider the best. Given the lack of general public knowledge about the candidates in any political battle, votes must be based significantly on reputation, because they certainly aren't based on political platforms.

Franchising is a way for one totally new restaurant to piggy-back on the reputation of another restaurant. When the second location shares owners and chefs that's one thing, but when 10,000 locations exist worldwide, like McDonald's, the restaurants become copy/paste versions of a successful formula. Customers will eat at one location of McDonald's just as readily as they will visit a location they have never seen before, based on the reputation of the entire network of restaurants. If a new restaurant opened that somehow sold McDonald's food under a different name, it would have to build its customer base from scratch because no one would "know" anything about it.

We are programmed by evolution to look for leadership. Even leaders are attracted to other strong leaders who display value. When valuable people exist in an environment that supports their value it can be almost infectious. Similarly, when leaders exist in an environment that doesn't support their leadership, mutiny can be the result as followers begin to choose sides.

By understanding the way value works you can recognize opportunities to build it and the weaknesses in yourself that you can improve.

TRY THIS AT HOME

So what, exactly, does a valuable person do? For those readers who want the checklist of valuable behaviour I can offer you a summary of how the best persuaders behave, and then you'll be on your own to put a personal spin on it. However, I must say, that if you are looking for too much instruction on valuable behaviour then you're trying to imitate it rather than doing it. It should be easy to see these traits in people you admire, so that could be a great place to start.

Understand value and believe in it.

If you have understood what you have read in this chapter so far, you're on your way. But you must not only understand it, you must believe it. Once you do, confident behavior will begin to emerge all on its own. Most people have some scenario in life where they feel their own value. Academics, sports, with friends, alone, playing World of Warcraft, doing people's taxes, cleaning your house... whatever. Think of how you feel in "your element" and how you would feel if you were demonstrating that to other people. Then apply that valuable feeling and that valuable behavior to the rest of your life.

Relax.

Let your body language tell how you feel. Shoulders down, back, and loose. Breathe normally. Walk like you're satisfied or proud, and only concern yourself with things that matter. Be aware of whether you are acting out of confidence, interest, and curiosity, or whether you're being defensive, fearful, and insecure. Decisions based on negative feelings are often negative decisions. Everyone is insecure about something; learn to leave it out of your decision-making. Just relax and ask yourself what a confident valuable person would do.

Be decisive.

Consider your options and make a choice. Ask questions and admit when you don't know the answer. Be responsible for your actions, but believe in your choices. Leaders know that even a wrong decision is better than no decision, and they feel confident to be the person actually making that decision. If you discover a decision was actually wrong, or if someone else brings you new information, be confident enough to change your mind... just make sure you're changing your mind out of confidence, not doubt or social pressure. Be sure, then do it. Once a decision has been made, own it.

Never feel threatened. Ever.

You are valuable, and other valuable people only enhance your value, so support them and welcome them. If they have a better idea, a better car, or a more attractive spouse, great for them! What does that have to do with you? Your social value is not connected to your value as a professional, or the value of your bank account, or the value of other people. Learn to take criticism with grace. I will admit that – as a creative professional – this has been challenging for me at times as well, but worth it.

Edit your emotions.

When a pick-up artist gets the green light from a beautiful woman, they take it in stride. When James Bond is threatened by a villain he appears cool and calm. When a comedian is under pressure to be funny for a stadium full of people, they deliver with confidence. When a talented potential employee interviews for a job they seem focused rather than nervous, because they expect more than one offer.

It can be tempting to get carried away when presented with a fantastic opportunity. As soon as you let your emotions take over your behavior, you're demonstrating that this is a big deal for you, which reduces your value to people that have experienced it before. Act as if you have done this before instead. You still like it and enjoy it, but it's not *spectacular*. If you rush into an attractive situation, you lose value. On the other hand, if you are pleased but under control (maybe even resisting a little), people assume it is a normal occurrence for you. This is called indifference, and will be a valuable tool in Step 3 and Step 4.

Maintain your value, always.*

Other people may also attempt to "test" your value by challenging it. You can handle it, and you're not threatened. An interrogator would never walk into an interrogation thinking "gee, I hope this criminal respects my authority." Even if the criminal doesn't, the interrogator never falters. He's in charge and everyone knows it, *especially* if the criminal challenges. Pick-up artists call it a "shit test" when a woman tries to challenge the PUA's leadership in the conversation, because she's checking for bullshit.

For example, a PUA will rarely buy a woman a drink (because it lowers his value), and if she asks for one, he will make her earn it instead. A low-value person might be happy that she has asked to have a drink purchased for her, but a Pick-Up Artist realizes that he is winning. If he buys the drink he loses, because she is testing his value. By making her earn it, he is testing hers, and the person granting approval is the one pulling the strings. The higher the value of a person, the more valuable you have to be to get their attention. The more you work for someone's attention, the lower your own value becomes (relative to theirs). Valuable persuaders always maintain their value, but remember – they never feel threatened. If she wins the drink, she wins the drink. And she can get the next round.

* = It is possible to demonstrate so much value that the other person feels unworthy, or uncomfortable, or embarrassed for even wanting to be near you. For example, if a young basketball player were to meet Michael Jordan, and Jordan played hard-to-get, he might seem mean, because his value is so far above the young player. The best thing to do when you wield significant value over someone else, is to give a little slack. Being "too valuable" may seem like a luxurious problem to have, but be aware that it's possible. When someone is excited to be around you – like when people fall in love – it is beneficial to switch gears (at least occasionally) when you recognize it. In persuasion it is usually more important to be relatable than it is to be powerful.

Be Enthusiastic.

Have you ever heard someone say they appreciate it when someone is passionate about something? It's very true. People enjoy interacting with someone who genuinely gets excited about what they do, and enthusiasm is contagious. Enthusiastic salespeople sell more because customers get wrapped up in the excitement of the sale. Religious evangelists are notoriously enthusiastic. Plus it is a little more difficult to say no to someone who genuinely loves what they are explaining.

After reading about editing your emotions you may be a little confused to read about enthusiasm being persuasive and valuable. Editing your emotions doesn't mean being a robot, it just means to you keep yourself under control. To be passionate about something is valuable, because passionate people are driven, unstoppable, and successful. They don't pause to consider whether other people approve, understand, or agree; they just do what they love. Athletes, for example, are often overwhelmed with enthusiasm when they win.

Enthusiasm is not the same as fanaticism, or craziness, or trying to convince someone that what you like is worthwhile. Enthusiasm doesn't ask permission. Enthusiasm is pride, competence, and enjoyment, and those are very attractive qualities in any person.

In addition to these traits (which are common to all people), it may be useful to realize that men and women are perceived differently, and may want to show value differently in different situations.

Both genders have weaknesses and advantages, and both have certain biases when perceived by the opposite sex.

Men can "get away with" being much more stern and commanding than a woman can in general, but especially in some professional contexts. While a mean man is a ruthless leader, a mean woman can become a demanding bitch. Both genders can go too far, but "the line" is in different places.

Women, on the other hand, have the advantage of kindness. While a woman can be insightful, thoughtful, and "in tune" with people – especially when volunteering compliments – a man becomes "weak" sooner. Both genders can be a push-over or "spineless", but again, the limits are different.

Sexuality – whether in sexual situations or not – can also have different types of limits depending on gender. Men have an unfair advantage at times, but face a major risk if they push flirting too far in the wrong context. Woman are noticed for sexual elements very quickly and although it can cause negative reactions from other women, the risk of harassment issues is decidedly lower. For women, be careful not to mistake attraction for respect, because they rarely come as a package.

If your persuasion is gender-specific or sexual, use it. If not, think twice before playing the sexuality card in your value-creation.

AVOID MANIPULATION

There is always another side to persuasion, and that is manipulation. As we learned earlier, the steps and ideas of persuasion and manipulation are the same, but the intentions of persuaders and manipulators are different. When it comes to reputation, we must realize that persuaders aren't the only people that display value. There are a few quick red flags to watch for, and guidelines to follow to avoid being manipulated.

First and foremost, believing in your own value and acting with value will genuinely reduce the number of people who seek to use and abuse you. Valuable people never cling, or beg, or hope for other people to solve their problems. That closes most of the manipulative doors. Like the diamond in the fancy display, a valuable person knows that waiting for the right opportunity is much more valuable than taking the first opportunity.

Conversely, manipulators often display a great deal of value, which is what makes them so effective. However, while people with true social value show comfort and confidence, manipulators tend to prefer control and guilt as their tools.

We discussed the idea of a "follower" before, and an interesting thing happens when a follower and a manipulator get together. The reason the manipulator wants the follower around is because the follower supports the manipulator's image of themselves. The manipulator only likes the follower while the follower is supporting the manipulation, and as soon as they stop that support, defensiveness and feelings of threat or anger are the result.

Manipulators may resort to lies to cover their weaknesses, and they may treat their followers without compassion. A manipulator feels superior to their followers, while a true leader knows that a king without an army is no king at all.

If you suspect that you are being manipulated, the most sure-fire test is to suddenly become unavailable or resistant, and watch the reaction of the other person. If they seem supportive and try to accomodate you, they are genuinely persuading. However, if they become angry or try to blame you or make you feel guilty for their inconvenience, those are the marks of a manipulator.

Resisting a manipulator ruins their selfish plans, while resisting a persuader creates a loss for both of you, so they will want to help you solve the problem in a "win-win" sort of way.

We will learn to recognize the goals of manipulators and the deceptive elements of compensation in Step 2.

SUMMARY

Your parents were wrong; a persuader should care about what other people think.

Reputation:
A reputation is the accumulation of all the impressions a persuader has made on another person, whether that is a few seconds or decades. The key to creating a good reputation is to understand the way value works and is communicated.

Value:
Value is the combination of how much of something there is (scarcity), and how many people want it (demand, or social proof). *Believing* something is valuable *actually* makes it valuable for the believer. Value is perception, not cost.

Valuable Environments:
By surrounding ourselves with people and situations that support our persuasive value we can communicate value through our environment as well.

Valuable Behavior:

Understand value and believe in it, relax, be decisive, edit your emotions, never feel threatened, always maintain your value, and be enthusiastic.

Next, in Step 2, we will learn about the motivations that control all humans. By understanding those motivations a persuader knows what other people want before they do, knows when they're hiding something, and when to play hard-to-get.

STEP
02

Predict Your Audience

Understand what motivates people to agree.

EVERYONE ACTS OUT OF SELF-INTEREST, ALWAYS.

Many of the most predictive persuasive disciplines put effort into analyzing the people they persuade before the persuasion begins. And whether it is conscious or subconscious, all persuaders try to predict what the other person wants. Understanding how people think can give you a lot of control.

For example:

You just started breathing manually. You may notice that one foot feels warmer than the other. You will blink once or twice just after this sentence, but only after resisting it for a second.

Tomorrow morning you will use the bathroom not long after you wake up. Someone you work with has thought of you in a sexual way, but not someone you'd be interested in. You remember your first kiss well, but your second kiss is kinda foggy. You have your insecurities – who doesn't? – but you're more confident now than you've ever been. You've been through a lot and few people really understand that.

Friends have come and gone in your life, but the ones you have now are the ones that will be with you forever. And they are lucky to have you! They may not always say it, but they appreciate the little things you do for them (and the drama you put up with sometimes).

If these statements seem surprisingly accurate it's because I wrote this book specifically for you. You're welcome.

Marketers survey and profile their target audience to understand their culture. Fortune-tellers study demographics and the most common fears and worries. Screenplay writers create characters and storylines to affect a specific audience. Infomercial producers keep meticulous statistics of what sells and what doesn't. And for therapists, knowing which question to ask is essential.

Their goals are to find out what makes people tick and adapt their persuasions. Those persuasions, when done well, are generally more effective and take less time to create than "shooting in the dark" based on intuition. And they were repeatable. But not all professional persuaders have this step figured out.

The Reid Technique used in interrogation, for example, has more of a carpet-bomb approach which uses forceful, deliberate techniques. The result can be false confessions and unreliable information, because the suspect doesn't *want* to confess. It is merely their only choice.

Amateur persuaders often try to guess what the other person wants and then offer to trade. Kids are amusing to watch as they first ask for something, then get mad, and then offer something like this:

"If you let me _____, I'll do all of my chores right now!"

Note to readers: trying to negotiate with something you're supposed to do anyway is usually a bad strategy.

This seems transparent to adults because we already know what they are trying to accomplish. When a persuader understands the wants and needs of all humans, all persuasion becomes transparent in the same way. Especially with adults.

So what do people want? What motivates them to agree?

(Too) many researchers attempt to explain persuasion techniques based on personality. One thing that psychologists are reluctant to admit, however, is that – although there are many theories – nobody really knows what causes personalities. Psychologists don't even agree on what a "personality" is, and I suspect they never will.

Additionally, most people agree that in different situations their personality traits can change. Outgoing extroversion with friends becomes quiet introversion with strangers.

If we don't know what it is, and we don't know how it works, and it changes depending on context, there must be something better.

Personality types – psychological categories of people – were another option. As it turns out, they are closer to astrology than science. In fact, it was astrology techniques themselves that made me realize the similarities.

The "5-Factor Model" is only somewhat better, and even the most scientific personality research (studies of twins separated at birth) only accounts for 50% of behavior and suffers heavily from selection bias (noticing the exciting examples while ignoring the majority).

Personality types and traits are typically assessed by having a person fill out a form (an "inventory"), and then *repeating what they said about themselves*. It doesn't take a scientist to do that, and we will learn why asking people about themselves is unreliable later in this chapter. More importantly, persuasion can be successful without asking the other person what they want, so that can't be our only option.

Persuasion via personality tends to use a "bottom-up" approach by starting with minor details like someone's favorite food or sports team, and trying to use those details to guess how the person might react to something else. Not only does it take years to know someone that well, but the correlation between two unrelated behaviors is just your intuition, and hopefully this book will provide you with a long list of reasons why intuition is unreliable as well.

Many great persuaders are successful without knowing the other person at all, so this also can't be the method at the core of persuasion.

Using personality as a guide for persuasion could be compared to a doctor trying to treat a cough without knowing if it is the flu or lung cancer. The more effective approach would be to diagnose the illness, not individual symptoms.

So, rather than trying to attack every unique personality-based situation, I thought it would be wiser to look at the universal things that apply to all people. In theory, if all people persuade and can be persuaded, we must have something in common upon which persuasion can be built.

That approach turned out to be very productive.

What the research for this book uncovered is the fact that there are surprisingly few things that motivate all people, in all cultures. Only 14 things, in fact. And personality only effects the details of how someone satisfies those motivations (e.g. – everyone eats; whether they choose pizza or curry is not the point).

The sources for these motivations came from every persuasive direction available. Psychology and social sciences contributed a lot, as did persuasive professions, and even popular culture sometimes supplied the best examples. Although many sources agreed on these ideas, no one source alone provided a complete, reliable method. Of everything in this book, this list of motivations and their mechanics is the most "composite" element.

We will look at each motivation individually in this chapter, and how people try to hide them using *compensation*. At the end we will look at rules for using motivation, and even how it can affect your view of yourself.

WHAT ARE MOTIVATIONS?

A motivation is a feeling. A feeling that we want something (a "gain"), or want to avoid losing something (a "loss"). A motivation is not a thing. The motivation to get a trophy is the feeling of winning, not the trophy itself. This is a very important point and a very common mistake.

Many people have studied motivation before this book, and many of those people were influential.

In 1943, American psychologist Abraham Maslow originally suggested something called a Hierarchy of Needs which basically says: of all the instinctual needs or motivations that people have, there is a certain order in which they are fulfilled. We need air more than we need safety. We need safety more than we need love. We need love more than we need to be creative. I am oversimplifying the concept a little, but you get the idea. This is something that most books about decision-making and persuasion mention. Some needs are more important than others and we satisfy those first, given the choice.

Maslow's theory, however, was a little vague about was what those needs are, specifically. Instead he refers to categories of needs (physiological, safety, social/love, self-esteem, and self-actualization) that are fairly easy to grasp and observe in real people.

Douglas Kenrick and Steven Neuberg (2010), both ASU professors, published a paper in which they re-cast Maslow's iconic pyramid. The new pyramid listed needs (from highest to least priority) as physiological, self-protection, affiliation, status/esteem, mate acquisition, mate retention, and parenting. Their goal was supposedly to reflect real life more closely.

In the context of persuasion it would be extremely useful if someone would abandon one need in favour of another because they were on different levels in the pyramid. However, one issue with all hierarchies of needs is how easy they are to break.

The newer hierarchy tries to address this by admitting that a person doesn't always stay in a higher level just because they had satisfied the lower level, hence the dotted (rather than solid) lines in the diagram. However, they still stuck with the general principle of one type of motivation "overruling" another. Although it is definitely *closer* to real life, and uses more recent science, there are still far too many opportunities to break that model.

If someone is deprived of something they need for long enough, or if someone is offered enough of something they want, they will readily ignore those "more important" needs on lower levels of the pyramid. If I offer you a million dollars and all you have to do is stay awake for a week, you'd probably do it. I would. And most people would give up food and sleep (and a little safety) to take a 10-hour flight to see a loved one. They would be cranky, but they'd do it.

If the highest part of the pyramid is the least priority (only satisfied after all others), why will people die for their children or

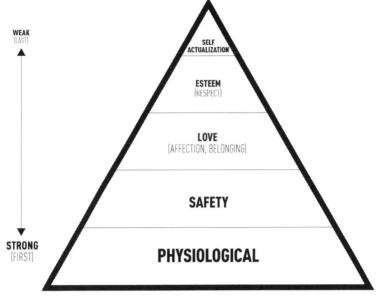

MASLOW'S HIERARCHY OF NEEDS (1943)

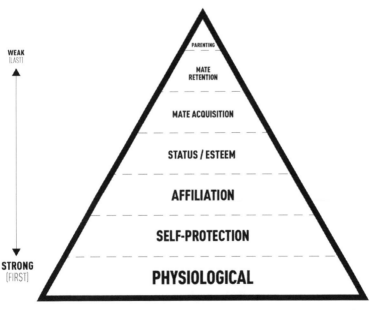

KENRICK & NEUBERG'S HIERARCHY OF NEEDS (2010)

their religion or their art? And if death and physiological needs are the most sacred, no one would ever commit suicide. Sadly, many do.

In actuality Maslow, Kendrick, and Neuberg probably intended their hierarchies to represent normal needs under normal conditions and it probably isn't fair to challenge them in such ways. However, all hierarchies aside, the actual needs that both sets of research had in their pyramids are much more interesting, persuasively speaking. But we need something a little more specific.

Desmond Morris, a zoologist famous for studying humans as if they were wild animals, has also argued that we base most of our life choices on evolutionary priorities. While some of his theories are becoming dated, the basic principle is easy to observe in real life. Evolution has built us in a certain way, and it has built us all in the same way (give or take). His work suggested a more specific list of motivations, and I think he was on the right track.

In 2000 and 2004 Professor Steven Reiss published complementary papers which attempted – yet again – to identify which needs, specifically, humans have. He profiled 6000 people and found that all of their daily activities could be reduced to 16 motivations. While I would say that some of his 16 motivations are a little poetic (honor, tranquility) he definitely narrowed the scope.

One of Reiss' proposed motivations, for example, was a need for physical activity. Considering the obesity problem in many western countries, it doesn't make a great candidate for a universal motivation. Even better, it can be explained in a different way by the motivations in this book.

Along with Maslow's concepts and Kendrick/Neuberg's concepts, Reiss's research gave an interesting 3rd point of view (with some adjustments to each).

Although psychologists usually have to work with only a few people at a time (or a few thousand if they're well-funded), I come from the world of Internet statistics where we can gather data about 10's of thousands of people in a matter of hours (or minutes!), with very little chance of accidentally creating bias in the results (everything is handled by computers). If we were trying to profile the entire human race, I wanted some very serious evidence to be convinced.

For this book I looked for the motivations that all people share in some form or another, and that are represented by major aspects of human society. Then I made sure that those behaviors were consistent with biology and could be observed on a personal level. It took almost three years, but eventually it was exciting to have something so reliable.

This motivation-based method of analyzing persuasion is easier, more predictable, and more specific than any of the research based on personalities. It re-organizes motivations based on *complexity*, not importance. I propose that we satisfy basic motivations before complex ones, merely because it is easier. But if provoked, we will satisfy any motivation at any time, in any order. All motivations can be irresistable from minute-to-minute interactions to major life decisions and preferences.

Additionally, this model of motivations allows for unconventional scenarios, like satisfying two motivations at once, or resisting a lower motivation for a higher one. Hierarchies make it very difficult to work with those kinds of situations in theory, even though they happen daily in real life.

Since anything can grab our interest at any time, motivations tend to compete for our attention. The more provoked or available they are, the more likely we are to act to satisfy them. This type of internal competition follows a few simple rules, which are important for actually using motivations. They will be discussed in the "Try This at Home" section of this chapter.

If you're feeling skeptical about how so much complexity in so many lives can be explained with so few motivations, you're normal. Many people resist the idea, because of our motivation for Status, which we will discuss later in this step.

THE 14 CORE MOTIVATIONS

Self-Preservation
>1. Avoiding Death
>2. Avoiding Pain

Physiological
>3. Air
>4. Water
>5. Food
>6. Homeostasis
>7. Sleep

Familial
>8. Sex
>9. Love
>10. Protection of Children

Social
>11. Status
>12. Affiliation
>13. Justice

Meta-Motivation
>14. Understanding

Throughout this book, motivations described in examples will be noted like this: *(Motivation)*.

Here I will describe each of the 14 motivations and some of the ways people commonly satisfy them. They will all be familiar in theory because (I assume) you are a human, but you may be surprised how counter-intuitive many of them are in practice. As you read, keep in mind that every persuasion you ever do, for the rest of your life, will

COMPOSITE
MODEL OF CORE
MOTIVATIONS

(2011)

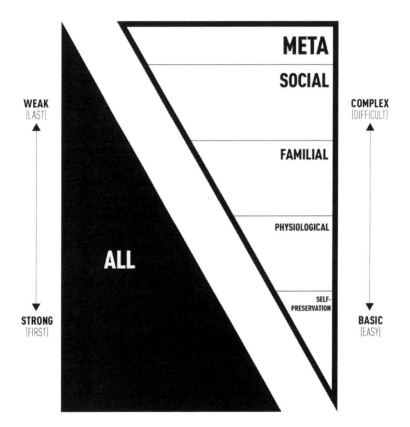

META

SOCIAL

FAMILIAL

PHYSIOLOGICAL

SELF-PRESERVATION

ALL

WEAK
(LAST)

STRONG
(FIRST)

COMPLEX
(DIFFICULT)

BASIC
(EASY)

involve one or more of these motivations. After we examine these truly universal motivations we will look at several pseudomotivations that are motivational wolves in sheep's clothing.

Self-Preservation Motivations
Avoiding Death (#1) & Avoiding Pain (#2)

Anyone who has touched something hot is aware of how basic and reflexive self-preservation is. Animals, including humans, will immediately try to escape or eliminate a threat when their lives are in danger, and we will pull our hands back instantly when our nerves detect damage.

One example of self-preservation that I have always found interesting is when a murderer is sentenced to be executed.

On a practical level, serving multiple life sentences without parole versus being sentenced to death row are exactly the same, except one allows you to stay alive. They both take your life, but one takes it literally, and one takes it figuratively. In other words, one scenario acts on your motivation for self-preservation *(Avoid Death)*, and one doesn't. Guess which one evokes fear and ethical debate...

Universal motivations cause people to want things with or without a rational explanation. You could say that death row provides the criminal with a quick and relatively easy way out, whereas multiple life sentences mean only mild suffering for the rest of the criminal's life. A death sentence doesn't necessarily sound worse to me, although if I were put in that situation my opinion might change.

Avoiding Pain deals purely with physical pain. Emotional pain, like the loss of a loved one, comes later. For now we are dealing with things like broken bones, puncturing your skin and organs, and extreme amounts of temperature, noise, light, etc. (your inner ear and eyeballs are the most sensitive parts of your body). Anything that hurts. And the more it hurts, the more motivated we feel to make it stop.

Although very similar to death, avoiding pain has a slightly different character. A person can be hurt many times, and in different amounts, whereas once you're dead, you're dead.

We will not only work hard to prevent these conditions, but will also surround ourselves with the most comfortable environment possible. Soft blankets, pillows, and beds while we sleep. Comfortable clothing, cars (with air conditioning), and furniture. And so on.

Self-preservation is focused on *prevention* because we normally exist in a state of comfort and being alive. The unique thing about these motivations is that we are motivated *not* to die or feel pain, so a "gain" means not dying or not feeling pain, and "loss" means dying or feeling pain.

Obviously we should not resort to threats of bodily harm to get what we want. Those are the methods of desperate people and criminals. But it is worth recognizing that when forced to choose between pain or death and some other unpleasant act, people will almost always choose the unpleasant act.

Physiological Motivations
Air (#3), Water (#4), Food (#5), Homeostasis (#6) & Sleep (#7)

These motivations occupy the majority of our time each day, and are concerned with keeping our bodies in good operating condition. With a few minutes of thought, it might surprise you how much of our culture, business, and social expectations are built around these simple motivations.

If a person is choking or being choked *(Air)*, you will see them suddenly spring into action to do anything they can to eliminate the cause. Even perfectly healthy people will panic and try to escape from thick smoke or noxious air-born chemicals like tear gas, which is used to disperse crowds. Air is something we need constantly, and something we have constantly. It is difficult to motivate someone to improve their air supply unless the supply is limited. This type of persuasion may involve things like scuba gear, air purifiers, or allergy medication.

Our bodies need constant replenishment of fluids *(Water)* because we can only live for a few days without water. People lost in the desert want water so badly they begin to imagine sources of it. Realistically the average person will have a drink of something several times per day, and will be quite motivated to find fluids when thirsty.

The industry built around beverages, for example, is absolutely massive. In the wealthiest countries there are shelves upon shelves of beverage options, and many of them actually make you *more thirsty*, like soft drinks and alcohol. In rural areas or developing countries, entire villages are built around sources of fresh water. The instinctual desire to put something wet in our mouths can become overwhelming after only hours without a drink.

Grocery stores, restaurants, and organized meal times are all symptoms of our need to eat regularly *(Food)*. The need for water may be more serious, but the need for food is often more distracting. Hunger can make people irritable and tired, can reduce our attention span, and can even create feelings of desperation. Anyone who has gone grocery shopping on an empty stomach knows exactly how persuasive hunger can be.

Motivation #6, *Homeostasis*, is the motivation to keep your body's processes running smoothly from beginning to end, so to speak. From vomiting to an urgent need for a bathroom, Homeostasis is obvious, common, and the need can become serious, quickly. Although homeostasis seems like an unusual motivation to use in a typical persuasion, I would never presume to foresee all of its potential persuasive uses. If you sell toilet paper, you probably know exactly what I mean. Charging a fee to use a public bathroom is strictly manipulation in my mind, but it is the norm in many countries. The alternative to paying the fee is is public embarrassment *(Status)*, because our bodies will not take "no" for an answer.

Motivation #7 is *Sleep*, and every mammal sleeps. Some at night and some during the day, but we all do it. After 24 hours without sleep a person becomes pretty much useless and after a week our immune system resembles someone who is pre-diabetic. When we get tired it is a downward spiral. First our attention span begins to get shorter, we become irritable, and we daydream. The longer it has been since we slept the more another motivation has to step in and keep us awake. Eventually we will fall asleep regardless of our situation, even if we're driving at full speed on the highway. A lack of sleep is even an effective form of torture or coercion, making people very suggestible.

Motivating people via Physiological Motivations is usually a matter of playing with their senses to create desire, or by restricting access to these necessary things. Advertising is famous for "selling the sizzle" of food, which can make your mouth water just through imagery. The sound of cracking open a cold beer at a barbecue can be enough to make people want to join in. On the other hand, our friendly neighbourhood cinema controls access to beverages, food, and bathrooms all for the sake of their own profit, which would be manipulation if not for the movie experience we get in return.

From hotels and restauarants, to diapers and oxygen tanks, to bottled water and travel pillows, we ensure we have these motivations covered everywhere we go, at all times. And businesses will rush to our aid wherever and whenever they can. The strategies for satisfying these motivations are ubiquitous, basic, and very useful in many persuasions.

Familial Motivations
Sex (#8), Love (#9), and Protection of Children (#10)

Motivations 8-10 deal with making kids, raising kids, and protecting kids and each can be powerfully persuasive on their own.

The first 7 motivations were based on a physical need for staying alive. If you need food, you eat. If you're tired, you sleep. If you're dead, everything else is somewhat irrelevant.

Sex isn't like that. And sexual attraction can seem like a mystifying condition for almost everyone. But let's deal with sex itself first.

A person can survive perfectly well without ever having sex; it is not based on any direct physical necessity. Motivations 8-14 all have this in common. However, without sex our species would become extinct very quickly. The solution that developed via evolution is a reward of extreme pleasure. We want sex because it feels good, but we don't just want sex with anything. We want someone attractive.

So what makes someone attractive?

Men and women can both be completely confused by the opposite sex, but nobody ever considers themselves confusing. The reason is very simple: men and women are attracted by different things, but we assume the opposite sex wants what we want. The result is that the harder we try, the less it works.

For example, although traits like "good sense of humour, sensitive, and supportive" show up on surveys of what women find attractive, those qualities don't actually match what women choose. It does, however, match who they choose as friends and resembles the traits women tend to value in themselves *(Affiliation)*. Ah, what complicated webs we weave.

There is more than one opinion in academic circles about why and how sexual attraction happens, and in my opinion this is because sexual attraction is difficult to observe without ruining it and nearly impossible to recreate in a lab. And scientist types – dare I say – don't tend to be master seducers by nature. However, pick up artists (PUA's) have literally made it their business to find the most effective ways to seduce women, and their methods can be reverse-engineered with science. They have not only deciphered exactly what women want, but also what the pick up artists themselves want, because resisting your own urges is the first step to becoming sexually attractive as a man; the opposite is true as a woman.

A basic difference between men and women begins to unravel the confusion: women can get pregnant and men can't. In terms of evolution, that makes a big difference.

Men are motivated to have sex with any woman that possesses fertility, health, and youth. All the qualities that make reproduction more likely. Fashion, make-up, and even plastic surgery are all used to make a woman seem more youthful, for better or worse. It is important to note that it is not *actual* youth, fertility, and health that achieve these results, just the traits of those things.

Women, on the other hand, must choose their sexual partners carefully. One roll-in-the-hay can create babies that take a lifetime to raise. Woman are generally attracted to a man whose traits show a woman that her babies will be strong, protected, and most likely to survive. This is so common in nature it's almost boring, but for some reason we have a hard time admitting that humans are the same.

The best evidence of what triggers attraction (if you're not convinced by science or PUA's) is who people choose to be unfaithful with. Afterall, it must be worth some level of risk to make someone cheat, right?

Men who cheat on their partners choose younger, more submissive, more adventurous women, who support the man's sexual role as the dominant, protective, competent partner. Their personality traits include confidence, an energetic attitude, and sexual freedom. Woman who cheat on their partners choose older, more dominant, more successful men who support the woman's role as the youthful, sexually-charged, submissive partner. Their personality traits include confidence, a selective indifference, and enthusiasm. Both choose a partner that emphasizes their attractive traits.

Note that "dominant" does not mean "controlling" or "superior", and "submissive" does not mean "weak" or "inferior". Strong sexual relationships, like any team, are built from a good balance of traits.

Women play hard to get when they are attracted to a man, because that is what attracts a woman; it seems natural to them. Men go for the gold when they are attracted, because that is what attracts them; again, it seems natural. The key to creating attraction for both genders is "playing cat-and-mouse." Show some interest, then show some indifference. The more attractive the person we are wooing, the more indifferent we must seem, which is explained in Step 4. The less attractive someone is, the more we can be up-front, because they need to feel more sure of success before they make a move. This is especially true for men.

Although Pick Up Artists can quickly and repeatedly demonstrate that this motivation is true (and I have tried it myself), the psychological community seems reluctant to admit it. I have even read research that proposes the exact opposite: the man that works hardest, gets the girl. It's just not true, it's not observable to be true, and it is not consistent with the rest of the animal kingdom.

It made me wonder if that conclusion represented wishful thinking on the part of the scientists themselves.

Love (motivation #9), tends to revolve around gaining and avoiding loss of the 14 motivations, but for another person. I have put several related ideas under the motivation "Love" for the sake of simplicity, although neurobiologists will tell you, correctly, that they are actually distinct processes in the brain.

There are three forms of Love: Parental Love for a child, Romantic Love for a mate, and Love for Family and Friends.

Parental Love is a motivation that every parent will recognize: the motivation to care for a child that is ours. I have been careful in the way I phrased that, because it is not only the motivation to be a parent, but to *care for* a child that is *ours*.

With motivations, these subtle nuances can effect the way we think about their mechanics and apply them in persuasion, so it is important to understand the difference.

In the 2010 Hierarchy of Needs they placed "parenting" at the top because they perceive it to be the weakest need. I particularly disagree with that aspect of the new pyramid, because – as anyone who creates algorithms knows – that arrangement would mean that very few people would ever "make it" to the top and have kids. And those that did would be so preoccupied with other things that their kids would be forgotten most of the time.

Parents with adopted kids or step children can become as attached as if they were biologically related. The child becomes "ours" even if it biologically isn't. Emotional "ownership" of a child is more about family closeness than genetics.

Romantic Love is the motivation to "pairbond" with a mate and provide them with the 14 motivations. We desire not only to love, but to be romantically loved in return.

This kind of Love has motivated songs, poems, stories, movies, plays, and television shows, ever since those things have existed. It has been compared to insanity a million times, because people will do unfathomable things to try to get, keep, or save a relationship with the person they love. That is probably the reason why Kenrick & Neuberg consider "getting a mate" and "keeping a mate" separate needs, although I wholeheartedly disagree. All motivations include gain and loss, and Love is no different.

Losing romantic Love comes with terrible heartache, and people are strongly motivated to avoid that loss, but not as a separate motivation. Finding romantic Love and avoiding the loss are two sides of the same coin.

Although Sex and Love have obvious connections, they are not the same. Men prefer different attributes in a woman depending on the amount of commitment the relationship will have: the face is their measurement of beauty in general, but the body plays a bigger role when sex is the only objective. Women prefer a supportive man as a husband, and a dominant man as a sex partner. Clearly there are separate mechanics at work. If sexual attraction and romantic love are the goal, different strategies apply at different times.

As Dr. Phil once said, "when the sex is good it's 10% of the relationship, and when it's bad it's 90% of the relationship." And who would argue with Dr. Phil?

Love for Family and Friends is not exclusive like Romantic Love and over a lifetime we tend to add friends into that inner, familial circle of love.

I am not aware of a way to measure love objectively, but I would suggest that the love of a parent for their child is stronger than vice versa, even if both can be strong. Children have much less trouble leaving their family for school or work than parents do saying goodbye.

Some families are very close, and others are distant. Some barely interact with each other. Lifelong friends seem as close or closer to us than blood-relatives, and we care for the well-being of friends and family in more-or-less the same way.

Protection of Children, Motivation #10, is an interesting motivation that is fairly easy to observe, but equally easy to overlook. It is basically a feeling of concern for any child, or anything with child-like qualities. Anything we might call "cute" or "adorable" can evoke this motivation.

It includes everything from trying to protect children from sexual predators on the Internet to letting them off first when a ship sinks. There are rational reasons for these things of course, but we're considering the *feeling* that motivates us to do it.

Us and baboons.

When a baboon needs to move through another group of baboons and feels threatened, it will carry an infant baboon with it as protection, and the other baboons will not attack for fear of hurting the infant. Humans feel the same way.

Major aspects of society are built around the protection of children, and many professions deal specifically with preventing young people from experiencing "loss" in the 14 motivations. Laws tend to evaluate children by different standards. And we do these things naturally, as individuals and as a community.

Even the worst criminals will bond together in prison over their hatred of pedophiles, and make sure the pedophiles get what they deserve *(Justice)*.

Social Motivations
Affiliation (#11), Status (#12), and Justice (#13)

When it comes to social groups, three motivations run the show. *Affiliation* is the motivation to belong to a group. *Status* is the motivation to improve our rank compared to the people around us. *Justice* is the feeling of what people "deserve" and is responsible for most of the conflicts between groups of people, like wars.

Affiliation is probably the simplest social motivation to observe. It includes ideas like belonging, acceptance, membership, following, trends, etc. Just go somewhere public and you'll see examples all around you, including yourself. At a major sporting event you will see people painted in their team colors and sitting on the "their" side of the stadium. And they have all paid to be there, supporting their Affiliation.

Humans are animals that need to live in groups, and our groups influence us a lot. We adopt each others' style of clothing, catch phrases, values, beliefs, and in extreme cases, identities.

A social group usually revolves around a dominant figure or a common interest, such as growing up in the same school or town, to being fans of the same sports team, liking the same music, working in the same office, etc, etc, etc. Anything in common can be a reason to form a "tribe".

Most people in modern society belong to many small tribes, unless they are a hermit or shut-in (in which case they're probably lonely).

Fashion exists for two reasons: one is sexual attraction and the other is to signify the tribes to which we belong (according to ourselves).

When we are outside a group and relate to its members, we will feel a strong desire to belong to that group. However, if one group is based on something that conflicts with the common interest of another group there will be a lot of animosity between the two groups *(Justice)*.

Interestingly, although we will adopt behavior of other people we want to be like, we will also build a group around ourselves, of like-minded people.

Affiliation also occurs in one-on-one situations. If someone says they "clicked" with another person or "felt at home" in a group, it is safe to assume that Affiliation is the underlying motivation.

During job interviews, favoritism is often shown to candidates that are most like the interviewer, and many interviewers will blatantly admit that they only hire people who "fit within the values of the company". Companies don't have values; people do. Whether interviewers realize it or not, they mean their own values.

Traditions are based on Affiliation as well, and can be quite persuasive. If you are a person who has always celebrated Christmas, imagine celebrating Hanukkah or Kwanzaa instead this year. Seriously. Even if Christmas has little to do with Christianity for you, the idea of celebrating it with another holiday procedure might immediately seem uncomfortable, and maybe even insulting. It wouldn't be unusual if the thought made you just a little bit sad.

If you try to explain why you feel this way, you will undoubtedly get trapped in circular logic like "because we're not Jewish!" which is the same as saying "we don't because we don't." There is nothing stopping you from being Jewish (assuming you're not Jewish). People convert to other religions all the time.

The point is not to question one religion against another, of course, but merely to demonstrate that when we are deeply ingrained in a strong "tribe" the idea of leaving that tribe won't even be an option in our minds, and to consider the possibility may provoke strong feelings, or even conflict.

Motivation #12 is *Status*. In a word, this is the motivation to be "better" than anyone and everyone around you. The word "Status" can have a negative connotation like "snobby" but that is only one version of Status. Every time you have felt good because you were promoted, or because you won something, or because you received a high grade or award, Status was responsible.

There are several ways to gain status including (but not limited to): Dominance, Affiliation, Sexuality, Competence, Autonomy, and Attention.

Dominance includes anything from power and authority to control and abuse, but in social science it usually isn't a negative word. It can be a very positive strategy as people strive for success in any chosen field. While men tend to exercise their dominance in a way that makes them most powerful, like in politics or business, women tend to exercise their dominance in a way that makes them most important or most envied, as in fame or an exclusive lifestyle. There are plenty of exceptions to that idea, but as a general guideline, it seems to be the current trend.

If the result is to have an easier life, access to bigger or better things, or control over things and people that other people don't have – even just for a moment – it is an increase in dominance, and therefore Status.

If the result is to have a harder lifestyle, smaller or worse things, or having less authority than other people – even just for a moment – it is a loss of dominance.

We will refuse to believe that our bad decisions, ideas, or actions could be responsible for a loss in Status until we are absolutely forced to accept it. The most common term to describe this is "denial." We will look at this more later in this chapter when we examine *compensation*.

Affiliation is another way to gain Status, if you are affiliated with the right people. Kevin Federline emerged from obscurity to become one of the most infamous celebrities in Hollywood, just by marrying Britney Spears.

The next best thing to dominance is to be associated with something dominant: a winning sports team, a popular rock band, an exclusive neighbourhood, the most-feared street gang, etc.

People are more likely to vote for a political candidate that they think will win, even if they disagree with some of their policies. Many people have become famous and powerful based on their criticism of high-value things, like food critics. It is common to hear people "name-drop" when they are affiliated with someone or something important, especially when they have no credibility or value otherwise.

Sexuality is the strategy of "if you've got it, flaunt it". This is a particularly useful strategy for women. From prostitution to "trophy wives" to free drinks and no cover charge, examples of this approach are easy to find. Men can absolutely use it as well, but the advantage is with the women.

People who are attractive during their youth often learn to use that as a strategy for Status. It can be very effective. As they age though, many people will go to incredible lengths to preserve their sexual advantage. Without it, it can feel like a huge loss, and sometimes even pain and suffering are worth the cost to re-gain a piece of that strategy. Not everyone focuses so heavily on one strategy, but if they do, it makes a persuader's (or manipulator's) job much easier.

Gaining Status via Competence is much simpler and potentially more powerful than either dominance or affiliation but there's a catch: you have to be good at something. Since competence can be directly related to your future potential, people are quick to notice and rally around a display of talent.

Shows like American Idol draw thousands of people each year, most of whom have little or no singing competence whatsoever. During the early episodes of an American Idol season we see excellent example after excellent example of how strongly people will resist the idea that they have lost Status due to a lack of talent. Interestingly, we respect people a little more when they admit their flaws, and fail with grace.

Competence can even transcend other core motivations, like Affiliation and Justice! The Red Baron was a talented WWI pilot who shot down many Allied pilots. He was technically the enemy, yet his outstanding competence in air combat won him the respect of his fellow soldiers and enemies alike. When he was finally shot down, his body was given a full military burial ceremony – by his enemies! High-ranking soldiers carried his coffin and he was saluted as a "worthy foe".

As far as Status strategies go, I find Autonomy very interesting. Autonomy is self-authority, or the ability to make choices for yourself. Some might call it "freedom" if it concerns grander things.

But there is another interesting dimension to autonomy that we see everywhere: if people are motivated by Autonomy and they face a barrier, they may adopt a completely different path in order to be autonomous. Entrepreneurship (working for yourself instead of others) is a positive example, and any form of rebellion is a (potentially) negative example. Children are often most motivated to do things that are prohibited, such as using a toy that is being used by another child. As soon as they are allowed to play with it, they no longer want to. Any type of exclusivity can have this affect, especially on adults.

Responsibility in general can include a dose of autonomy, and in many companies autonomy is a reward for good performance (as it should be). Some studies of corporate management have shown that increasing autonomy produces better results than increasing salary. Sometimes the gain of autonomy can outweigh the risk of incompetence, and people will jump at the opportunity to make their own choices, even when failure is more likely.

There is one *pseudostrategy* for Status that tends to have negative results when pursued for it's own sake, and that is: *getting attention*. Most people understand that important people draw more attention than unimportant people; this is just a fact of the matter. Thousands of people will gather to watch a highly competent performer, for example, and that attention is positive and deserved.

However, there is a segment of the population, including children, that associate the attention itself with being a gain in Status. Being sick, disruptive, hurt, or sad are all negative conditions that get sympathy attention, and some people will "play it up" to get more. Both adults and children may try to gain Status by doing things that

110

attract attention, even if that attention is negative.

"All PR is good PR." Not necessarily.

Ultimately the result is that someone becomes well-known, but rather than being well-liked, they are generally disrespected. Those who try the hardest are often least secure in their offer.

Occasionally we see someone turn that negative high-status into genuine high-status, but more often than not it is just a stressful, low-value way to be in the spotlight. Attention-seeking celebrities are reliably the ones in rehab or scandals. According to everything I have researched, attention-seeking behavior is an unreliable persuasive path to choose unless you are performing at the time (which is actually competence). Reality tv has generated millions of dollars by manipulating attention-seekers to look ridiculous on television.

Persuaders should gain attention from genuine importance, rather than merely being dramatic for its own sake, because a valuable person doesn't care who is watching.

Special Case: Affiliation + Status = Territorialism. Humans need personal space, like many animals. Even within a safe group we tend to be uncomfortable without any "breathing room". We usually extend our "territory" to include our homes, maybe our cars and offices, and our sales regions, and even our ideas and creative work. The key elements of territorialism are ownership and privacy *(Status)*.

In the most basic form of territorial behavior we protect what is "ours" including possessions and people. We often feel that losing some of our stuff is a personal loss, even though it's just stuff. If our house is broken into – even when we're not home and nothing is stolen – many people will cry.

A tribe has a territory as well *(Affiliation)* and those territories are much easier to observe. Countries have borders. Teams have "home court" advantage. Even family names signify who "belongs" to who. "Keep it in the family." When astronauts landed on the moon they planted an American flag which, when you think about it, is ridiculous. Unless you're American, then it may be a source of pride, because it "belongs" to the USA, apparently.

Persuading with territorialism is essentially persuading with Status or Affiliation, but it can be helpful to realize the boundaries between the two.

Justice (motivation #13) is the glue that holds civilization together. It includes morals and ethics, good and evil, right and wrong; fairness, karma, honor codes, and so on. You may also have heard other people describe it as "altruism" which basically means "doing good without personal reward", but that title ignores the negative side of Justice, which undoubtedly exists.

No one is entirely "good" or "evil", and when motivated properly, pretty much anyone is capable of pretty much anything. Justice makes sure people get what they "deserve", in the eyes of the tribe.

If someone eats our food out of the company fridge, someone must be held responsible. Or we can eat theirs tomorrow. We must maintain balance in The Force.

Justice works on the principle of *reciprocation*. When something unfair has occurred, doing exactly the same thing to the offender is now, suddenly, perfectly acceptable as a punishment. A killer is killed. A kidnapper becomes a prisoner. Outside the law, if one child teases another and the second child hits him, most observers will say "he had it coming" or "the other one started it." As adults we know that philosophy is wrong, but when its our kid, we're quietly happy that they gave that bully "a taste of his own medicine." Everything must be in balance, and not just with bad things. If someone lends you money you feel obligated to pay them back (unless another motivation is stronger).

Some persuasion researchers, such as Robert Cialdini, have claimed that any gift or favor creates this feeling of obligation. In real life that is easy to disprove. When I was a student I used to plan my grocery trips so they happened on "sample day" when the supermarket offered free food. It did not influence my purchases. If a mob boss does you a favor, you are in his debt because he will hurt you *(Avoid Pain)* if you refuse to do him a favor later, not because your moral compass tells you to get involved in organized crime. People just aren't that stupid (usually).

Reciprocity alone is not the motivation; we are motivated to create balance within our tribe *in accordance with the values of the tribe*. If someone is worth more to the tribe they get more, and vice versa, and we are motivated to keep it that way.

Even more interesting is that actions considered immoral are entirely actions that cause *losses to the other motivations*. And the order we have discussed them in this book – give or take – is roughly the order of seriousness with which we enforce our morals. Some examples will help clarify this idea:

1. If you kill someone or assault them physically *(Death or Pain)* that can punishable by death or life in prison.

2. Access to water, food, and general safety *(Air, Water, Food, Homeostasis and perhaps Pain)* are considered universal human rights by the United Nations.

3. Rape *(Sex)* is probably the next most serious crime after murder and even among criminals is considered distasteful.

4. Anything related to bad parenting *(Love, Protection of Children)* like abuse, kidnapping, or neglect usually creates very strong feelings from the public and carries heavy prison sentences.

5. Adultery *(Love, Sex)* can be a legally viable reason for divorce, however the punishment for it is usually harsher from your social circle than from the law. Still a serious social offence, however it is notably less severe than murder, or rape.

6. Crimes involving Status are generally those like fraud or slander where people try to gain by deceiving others, or reduce the status of someone else by lying or cheating.

7. Betrayal *(Affiliation)* is always a serious offence in any relationship. The more people you betray, the larger the punishment. Disloyalty at work will lose you a job. Treason – betrayal of a government – can be punishable by death.

8. A loss in *Understanding* (the next and last motivation)

113

doesn't usually constitute a crime. However, as soon as people feel like they are being left in the dark or lied to (restricted information), resentment builds. Interestingly, sometimes a person feels they *deserve* to know, for no other reason than they *want* to know.

It is very important to note how our sense of morals changes when we are talking about enemies, i.e. – people outside our Affiliation. They are no longer treated like people. They are opponents, and must be eliminated (literally or figuratively). We are proud of our armies when they exterminate enemies who are doing things that are morally unacceptable from our tribe's point of view. But when we feel as if we belong to the tribe that is being exterminated, every member of our tribe becomes valuable. And both sides of a conflict feel the same, creating an endless cycle of conflict.

There are two key ingredients required to predict Justice: the value of a person to the tribe and the point of view we're considering. If it is their own point of view, they "deserve" almost anything they want. If it is their tribe's point of view, the rules and culture of the tribe dictates what they deserve. If it is an enemy tribe's point of view, much more is required to earn respect and reward, and it might even be impossible.

Meta-Motivation
Understanding (#14)

Understanding includes ideas like curiosity, evaluating, interest, and closure. We just need to know! Understanding is the need to evaluate or learn from an experience or situation, including the experience or situation of someone else. The first question when driving by a car accident is always "what happened?" and we are fascinated.

Understanding is motivating when it concerns the previous 13 motivations. The unique aspect of this is that everyone is interested in whatever they associate with core motivations through experience.

I call this *daisy-chaining*. For example, you might have persued football, while I am interested in programming, even though both are linked to Status. You might like pizza and I might prefer curry, but both are daisy-chained to our motivation for *Food*. Paying attention to someone's interests are the best way to figure out what they have daisy-chained to the core motivations, and therefore how to fine-tune our persuasions for them.

It can be very difficult to accept the fact that we are not allowed to know something *(Status, Justice)* or that there is no answer to our need for closure *(Love)*. If our leaders withhold information from us, we feel they have done us a disservice and we deserve to know *(Justice)*.

We also feel uncomfortable when the rules change so we don't understand anymore. This is a loss and we feel afraid or upset.

However, when observing someone else in a situation that doesn't affect us, we may calmly tell them to "let it go, man."

Like Justice, there are two ingredients in the motivation to Understand: motivations, and personal closeness. The bigger the gain or loss, the more we want to know. The more personally relevant it is, the more we want to know. If it is a huge gain or loss to someone close to us, we are *extremely* motivated to know.

There is one note to make about culture, for all motivations. Although all people experience all 14 motivations, different cultures (and even different people) may put different levels of importance on each motivation. For example, in the United States *Status* is considered very important, but in Sweden it is less important. In fact, in Sweden it is frowned upon to have too much more than you need. Taxes increase accordingly, and very few people are poor. Whereas the United States is famous for the American Dream; rich Americans are generally far richer than rich Swedes, and poor Americans are left to struggle. Likewise, Latin countries tend to put a high level of importance on Love and Food motivations, especially in combination. These differences are subtle, but they're there.

PSEUDOMOTIVATIONS

Motivations are feelings, not things (it's worth repeating). However, things appear to be motivating people all the time. Things may cause the feelings, via daisy-chaining, but it is the feelings that people want, not the things. If someone is motivated to enter a contest to win an iPhone, the persuader needs to know whether it is Status or Affiliation that does the trick, but the iPhone itself is irrelevant. The iPhone is a *pseudomotivation*.

There are a few pseudomotivations that are very convincing, but they're actually just disguising other motivations really well. You may have already noticed that these pseudomotivations were not on the list, and here is why:

Money is definitely the most deceptive pseudomotivator. It seems obvious: offer money, get results. Perhaps, but sometimes that backfires, which has perplexed researchers and managers for decades.

Currency is a symbol for buying power. We may be highly motivated to have money, but only so we can fulfill the 14 motivations. Money itself is *never* the goal.

You may be thinking – what's the difference? If it motivates, it motivates, right? True, but all of the 14 motivations can be fulfilled without money, and money is often the hard part. If you have the money to persuade, great! Take note that you want to use it for something already...

There is a common saying that money is "burning a hole" in someone's pocket. It is a "potential gain", waiting to happen. On the other hand there are people (a minority) who are constantly saving for a rainy day. These frugal folks may appear to be saving money for its own sake as well, but if you probe into their excellent saving habits you'll find that they are avoiding any number of potential losses in the future, namely lifestyle *(Status)*. They may find it stressful to spend money. The difference between wanting to spend or save money is merely whether you put more value on gaining or preventing loss, and both can be equally valid.

People aren't stupid; they know that money will get them what they want. However, that may cause them to treat money as if it is that motivation. Be aware of this, and use it wisely.

Health is a classic pseudomotivation. "At least you have your health." But what happens when you don't have your health? That depends, actually. If it is painful *(Avoid Pain)* or embarrassing *(Status)* then you'll have it treated. However, if it is neither of those things, most of the time it will go untreated or even unnoticed. Death isn't even motivating unless the risk is serious and urgent.

Most people forget to go to the dentist if there isn't a serious problem. A significant portion of North America and the UK is overweight. Think of all the smokers who kill themselves a little every day! Many people will stop taking prescribed medication when the visible symptoms disappear, even though some medications only work properly when you take the entire prescription. "I stopped taking the medication because it worked" is a great quote for demonstrating the non-motivational affect of health.

If your plan is to motivate healthier behavior for a condition that is neither painful, nor embarrassing, "health" and "longevity" are probably not going to do the trick.

Safety is another pseudomotivation that can be found in a number of motivation theories, but what *is* safety? If you have no risk of Death, no Pain and enough Air, Water, Food, Homeostasis, Sleep, Sex, Love, Affiliation, Status, Justice, and the Understanding to maintain stability in those things, I daresay you have an excellent life.

"Safety" is one of many elusive concepts that science (especially psychology) tend to provide us with – like "personality" – that are actually a collection of related ideas, and are hard to define in real life. It's a *category* of needs, not a need. Just like "privacy" or "shelter". The 14 motivations described earlier are what we fear losing, and if we seek shelter, privacy, or anything similar it is probably to avoid pain or embarrassment, and not merely to obtain "safety" for its own sake.

There are probably many more pseudomotivations, but with these examples as a guide, the main point is that motivations are feelings, not things, not categories, and not ideas to achieve for their own sake.

COMPENSATION

The idea of *compensation* is when someone thinks there is a chance of a loss, so they try to direct attention away from it, or hide it in general.

Lying would be the most blunt version, but it can be much more subtle than that. A typical example of compensation is when people start a sentence with "I don't want to be rude, but…" They are predicting that you might consider it rude if they say what they want to say, but they still want to say it. By adding that to the beginning of their thought, they are compensating.

There are endless ways people can do this. A Real Estate Agent might think the second bedroom is a little small, and to compensate they might volunteer suggestions about how you might create more storage in that room.

Nervous laughter is an excellent compensation signal. If a person feels socially uncomfortable, they may try to create humour to defuse their own discomfort.

Compensation is important because when a persuader notices compensation happening, it is a valuable piece of information: it identifies a motivation that is valuable to the other person at that moment, and is not being satified – an insecurity.

If someone feels socially nervous, they are afraid of social loss *(Affiliation, Status)*. By creating a gain for them – perhaps by inviting them into the conversation – the persuader is now the source of a social gain, and that is a powerful position to have.

If you notice someone compensating (everyone does eventually), take note of what they are compensating for, and add it to your mental list of persuasive tools. DO NOT tell them you noticed. It leads to conflict every time.

SELF-DELUSION

After exploring the 14 motivations that rule our lives we have arrived at the most important thing you will learn in this book. There is one overriding principle that effects all behavior:

Everyone acts out of self-interest, always.

It is true all the time, no matter what. All people, in every culture, everywhere. No exceptions, no special cases, no "super nice people" who somehow transcend evolution. If we can't understand how a person's action satisfies a motivation it does not mean it is an exception; we must investigate further.

If a person perceives no benefit for themselves in a persuasion, they are very unlikely to care, let alone agree. The benefits people are looking for are always some form of the 14 motivations. The most fatal mistake we can make in a persuasion is trying to cater to a sense of charity, generosity, or pity. It will almost always fail, because the definition of those things is giving something for nothing. The scenarios in which generosity or pity don't fail are – of course – when being generous creates a gain in one of the motivations.

For example, when a celebrity donates money or time for free they may receive Status, Affiliation, or Justice for their good deed. If you help a proverbial old lady cross the street, you feel good about yourself because you helped someone who deserved it *(Justice)*. If helping someone made us feel terrible every time, we would avoid it like the plague.

The idea that we do everything out of selfish motivation can

THE USE OF MONEY IS ALL THE ADVANTAGE THERE IS IN HAVING IT.

BENJAMIN FRANKLIN
AMERICAN SCIENTIST & POLITICIAN

strike some as a very cynical, narrow view of the world. However, whenever I have presented this to an audience and asked them for examples of situations that are totally selfless and are not based on the 14 motivations we discussed, I have never received a single valid suggestion. It can seem disheartening if you prefer to think that your generosity is a completely selfless decision. Ironically, even thinking that is motivated by self-interest, so it ends up being a nice example of this idea.

Rather than sit and think of reasons that people might act out of pure, selfless charity, why not do the opposite? What about all the negative things we may have been hurt by that actually weren't our fault? Every time someone broke up with you, every time someone has been mean to you, and every time someone didn't pick you for something fun, it was motivated by the other person's 14 motivations. You were merely collateral damage.

It's a little comforting, isn't it? Maybe. Maybe not, since we're arguing rationality versus emotion. Odds are, you know that it should be comforting, but it isn't. Luckily, the way we feel about something doesn't change whether it is correct or not.

Acting out of self-interest has one, huge side effect on all people and that is an inability to properly evaluate ourselves. We want to be unique, special, moral, well-liked, and full of potential, and since it is usually difficult to prove that we aren't, it happens to be very easy to believe that we are. Furthermore, everyone that agrees with us makes us believe it even more. Everyone that disagrees – well, they don't count.

Fortune Tellers use a technique called *Barnum Statements* which are carefully phrased to tell someone that they have two opposite traits, and the person will agree because they are both phrased as motivational gains. A variation on that theme is to tell people they have qualities that everyone wants to have, and about 90% of people will completely agree without hesitation. For example, I can tell that you are a person that values your private time, but when the right mood hits you, you can let loose and be the life of the party.

Unless you're a hermit, this is more or less true for anyone. But in person, with the proper inflection, it would sound remarkably personal and insightful.

Agreeing with what people already think about themselves is called *validation*. It is completely separate from, and completely unrelated to the truth, even if it happens to be true sometimes.

We won't go into all the details and techniques involved, but if you want to know more about fortune-telling techniques, I can recommend *The Full Facts Book of Cold Reading* by Ian Rowland, a professional 'mind-reader'. It is probably the best fortune telling book I have come across during my research and he explains everything better than I ever could.

So it is crucial to make these two points:

1) Everyone acts out of self-interest, always;
2) Never trust someone's evaluation of themselves, but always listen.

These give a persuader the ability to create a set of opinions that the other person will never disagree with. A fortune teller can tell you all about yourself, and you will be amazed at how well they know you. A psychologist can tell you all the quirky things about your personality and you'll be impressed with the accuracy of their "typology". You can write a term paper that repeats all the views and affiliations of your professor and they will beam with pride as they give you an A+.

On the other hand, if a persuader disagrees with the way someone sees themselves, even when backed with significant evidence, the persuasion suddenly gets stuck in the mud. From the other person's point of view, the persuader's credibility begins to fade, the trust between them disappears, and they begin to second guess whether the persuader is actually worthy (because there is no way the other person's self-image is wrong, that's ridiculous!).

Admittedly, this aspect of human behavior can be highly irritating, as someone will ignore a decision that is clearly the right choice, because doing so would admit some sort of difference between their self-image and the truth. In persuasion, it is the persuaders job to "re-frame" anything so it seems as if it is a gain, or a good quality to have, so the other person will agree willingly.

When faced with another person's self-delusion it can be a dirty problem. You can either disagree with them - which will appeal much more to your sense of Status and Justice – and face failure, or you can support their self-image and grease the wheels of the persuasion.

For example, if a potential client says "I have been in this industry for decades, so I know what talent looks like." Rather than telling them they are out of touch with modern practices, merely relax and tell them how comforting it is to have someone with enough experience to understand what you do *(Status)*.

The best part about this technique is that, because the person is already deceiving themselves, your clever re-framing will go completely undetected.

Some persuaders struggle with a feeling of soul-selling here, but creative persuaders can easily navigate self-delusion without compromising their principles. And you're more creative than you get credit for, I can tell. In fact, handling self-delusion well is the mark of a talented persuader, in my opinion, so it is worth working on. Just remember that the gain for you is biggest when your persuasion succeeds, regardless of how you got there.

TRY THIS AT HOME

All motivations follow a simple set of rules and by following these rules a persuader can use and abuse motivations on purpose, as well as predicting the way someone will react. All of these rules can be used at the same time (the more the merrier!), and can be applied to anything you want.

Create the possibility to gain or avoid loss.

A motivational gain is when someone satisfies a motivation more than it was satisfied previously. A motivational loss is when someone's motivation becomes less satisfied than before. For example, if you fall in love, that is a motivational gain *(Love)*. If that person breaks up with you, it's a loss *(Love)*.

Whether someone is gaining or preventing a loss is not as important as the fact that they can be motivated to do both.

The other person must realize that there is an opportunity for them to gain. It is best to let them realize it though, rather than spelling it out, because if the other person realizes they are being persuaded, it often cheapens the experience. Try to find the sweet spot between "hinting" and "explaining" so they understand, but don't think you're selling it too hard.

The fear of loss is equally – usually more – motivating. Be careful though, because the other person may resent you if they realize you're motivating them with veiled threats.

Try this: To witness the effect of a gain, find any reason to compliment someone. Don't lie; make it genuine. Put some effort into complimenting someone about a core motivation and watch how they brighten up immediately. Similarly, try saying something negative about someone without a reason, and watch the conversation dissolve instantly.

Allow gains to continue until risk outweighs gain.

When a person is gaining they will do so until/unless the opportunity to lose becomes more powerful. This is the "have your cake and eat it too" rule, and is often called greed when someone tries to gain too much.

A "freemium" sales model is the idea of offering a full product for free, and providing premium upgrades for a cost. It works really well for Google, among many others. However, many companies confuse freemium with offering a limited trial product for free and only offering the full product for a cost. Generally speaking, that just makes people abandon the product after forming a weak impression. A subtle but crippling difference.

It is also important to realize that it is the other person's assessment of risk that matters. If they think the risk is too high, it's too high, regardless of what the persuader (or facts) may say. Interestingly, once the risk of loss is removed the motivation to gain will usually still exist.

The fear of loss in one motivation can also influence the motivation to gain in a different motivation. A surprising number of people will keep the job they have even when a better option is available *(Status)*, because they like the people they work with *(Love, Affiliation)*. If you haven't eaten in days and you're offered your wildest sexual fantasy, you may choose to eat first anyway, assuming those are different things *(Food, Sex)*.

The persuader should provide the opportunity for the biggest motivation gain possible, minimize risk, and keep it comin'. Let them do it more. Let them do it again. Give them a photo to take home. Whatever.

Try this: Go through your monthly expenses and figure out how much you *should* be spending each month, like a minimum allowance. Put the rest of your money in a different account, and watch as you instantly reduce your spending, just because it is a pain-in-the-ass to get to your money. You have just eliminated many small, impulsive gains based on nothing but availability.

Use relative *gains and losses, not absolute.*

Motivations are based on having "more" or "less" rather than specific amounts. There is a classic game theory/psychology experiment that asks: would you rather make $90,000 per year and $5000 less than your colleagues, or make $85,000 per year and $5000 more than your colleagues?

In one scenario you make more money, in the other scenario you make less money. If you even pause to decide, that is your Status motivation making your intuition disagree with your rational thought. If salary is the only factor, it is irrelevant whether you are better or worse than your coworkers *(Status)*, but up to 70% of educated adults will choose to make less money as long as they make more than their co-workers.

It can even seem easier when it's a hypothetical situation, but if your employer offered you a raise that was smaller than everyone else's raise you would be upset, even though you are getting more money. Ask yourself: how, exactly, does another person's salary affect your life?

If your offer isn't particularly big or impressive, put something worse next to it. An unimpressive stereo looks good next to a crappy stereo. An average-looking person looks good next to an ugly person (especially if they look similar). An expensive package looks cheap next to a similarly-priced package with fewer features.

TIP: Subjective things are hard to compare like this. If you give me two colors to choose from and one of them is "obviously" better (in your mind), you can't be sure that my taste agrees with yours until I choose!

Designers make this mistake all the time, only to have the client choose the uglier option and fall in love with it. The really annoying part is that it was the designer who presented the ugly option in the first place, so they must admit it is ugly to persuade the client to change their mind.

"Everything is relative."

Try this: Find someone that owns something similar to you, but a lesser version. An older phone, a smaller car, non-digital cable... it doesn't matter what it is. Then trade with them for a week or three. Don't eliminate anything, just downgrade. Be worse on purpose, just to see how long it takes you to get used to it. You might be surprised how easy it is, even though you normally resist it.

Remember that motivation is automatic.
It is not a choice.

Human brains are wired by evolution. When we see something we want we might resist the motivation, but we still want it. And if we are resisting, resistance must be because we perceive a risk for pursuing that gain. Motivation is so automatic that most people are unaware of being motivated, even as they begin working towards the goal.

A persuader is often tempted to try to make someone be motivated. Marketers might be the worse example of this as they talk about "trigger words" that *make* people buy. Nonsense. A persuader must *allow* the other person to be motivated on their own. "Trying harder" has no effect at all, because the other person *cannot choose* to become motivated.

This is especially true in sexual seduction. Set the trap, then be confident enough to let the other person walk into it.

TIP: When you notice someone has become motivated, do not tell them. First of all, they won't understand what you mean, and second, you'll ruin your own persuasion. If you really want them to know why they are motivated, buy them a copy of this book.

Gains are easier to believe than losses. Use them first.

The lesson is: don't try to persuade by pointing out why someone "should" do differently, make them *feel* it.

For example, imagine you're fundraising for a charity and you are speaking to a potential donor:

"Charity is something we should all do. Anyone that can afford to give to charity has a moral duty to help those in need." That may feel good for the persuader *(Status),* but it is a subtle insult for the other person. You just told them they are amoral and that you are better.

Instead, you can show them how their current beliefs can match with your offer. "By donating, you are doing something exceptional for someone who really needs it, and we appreciate your donation more than you could ever know."

Same information, totally different feeling.

Like several other ideas in this book, some people will resist this, but the truth is that we believe a potential gain more easily than a

127

potential loss.

The second way of presenting it turns a donation into a gain of Status, because donating makes the other person "exceptional". The first way merely allows the other person to step out of the dirt and be not-selfish, but that means they must believe that they are already in the dirt.

When two people share taste in music or art, they immediately agree that both have good taste *(Status, Affiliation)*. If their tastes disagree, one or both will inevitably claim that the other has bad taste. Neither person will think that they are the one with bad taste because having bad taste when you thought you had good taste is a loss.

During persuasion the persuader must understand that people will bias their views of gain and loss in this way and to adjust accordingly (including the persuader!). Any opinions or judgements a persuader may have about these perceptions are irrelevant.

If it is possible to motivate with gains rather than losses, do it. It's easier for the other person to believe they are, or will be, as great as you say, rather than believing they are, or will be, less than they already believe.

Persuading someone to *avoid loss* is very effective. Persuading by *using* loss, is not.

AVOID MANIPULATION

There are two ways to be manipulated in this step: by other people, and by yourself.

If you manipulate yourself through self-delusion, there is nothing I can do for you. A competent persuader must learn to notice when they are hearing what they want to hear.

When your persuasions fail you may convince yourself that the method is flawed, or that the other person is just too dumb to understand, but be aware that both of those arguments make you the innocent bystander by default. If the method is wrong, find the flaw and fix it (and email your solution to me!). If the other person is dumb, then simplify your persuasion so they understand.

To be manipulated by someone else in this step is merely to let yourself stray down the path of "personality differences" or to believe the other person's compensation excuses. If someone is persuading you, realize which motivations you respond to most and give those a second or third thought before agreeing, just in case.

If someone threatens you with pain or death, do what they say. If they are trying to sell you something to prevent pain or death, ask yourself what their motivations might be, and choose wisely.

Physiological motivations are usually just a matter of thinking ahead. To avoid buying excessive food or beverages, have a little snack or bring some water. Go to the bathroom before you leave. Ask for a non-smoking room. Plan your stops so you're not falling asleep at the wheel. And so on.

Being manipulated by sex could probably be a book on its own. Women should avoid falling for men simply because they are unattainable, arrogant, or because they hold a higher position in life. Men should avoid thinking of women as the ones holding the power to give and withhold sex. Women should avoid the "dumb and helpless" strategy of creating attraction, because it sacrifices long term respect for short term attention. Men should avoid trying harder and harder to impress a woman, for the same reason. Relax, and be yourself!

Even the suggestion that your Love could be manipulated can be insulting. How can caring for a child or a pet be bad? The answer is either guilt or mind-reading.

If someone uses guilt to persuade you to do or buy something for someone you love, it is probably manipulation. It is common to make someone feel like they are a bad parent or spouse because they didn't spend enough or provide enough for their child or spouse, which is complete nonsense. If you are told that your infant child or pet wants you to buy something, that is just lying. Science has not discovered a way to speak dog or baby-talk, as far as I know, and "pet psychics" are

IT IS DOUBLE PLEASURE TO DECEIVE THE DECEIVER.

NICCOLO MACHIAVELLI
ITALIAN DIPLOMAT AND AUTHOR

absolutely full of it.

Social motivations are particularly easy to manipulate. If someone unwaveringly agrees with you, they might be benefiting from making you feel smart or accepted. Keep this in mind if you are the boss or a potential customer, especially. Only surround yourself with people better than you, and who are valuable. Being part of a group to make yourself feel superior may not be in your best interest. It may also be very difficult to resist.

Justice can be overwhelmingly motivational. Revenge will get you nothing, and you will always think other people will agree with your need for revenge more than they will. Also realize that you think your family and friends deserve more than other people, even if that isn't true. This can be a dangerous cocktail of motivations when someone is pushing your buttons or seriously betraying you.

The motivation to understand "why" can drive people to insanity. Closure may never come after a serious loss, but it can be unbelievably easy to obsess over it forever. And sometimes you're just not allowed to know for your own benefit. Know when to push and when to let it go.

And take time, alone, before making big decisions with any motivation. Give your feelings some time to settle down so you can think more objectively.

SUMMARY

We have covered a lot in this chapter, and that information will form the core of your persuasions forever. The main thing to take away from this chapter is that *everyone acts out of self-interest, always.*

Don't rely on personality:
Personality is not a reliable way to persuade people. Instead

we should use the 14 core motivations, which apply to all people everywhere. They are Avoiding Death and Pain, Air, Water, Food, Homeostasis, Sleep, Sex, Love, Protection of Children, Affiliation, Status, Justice, and Understanding.

Motivations:

Motivations are feelings, not things. We are motivated to gain something we don't have now, or to avoid losing what we already have. People will gain until the risk of loss outweighs the gain. Motivations are relative, not absolute. Motivation is not a choice, it is automatic. Gains are easier to believe than losses.

Pseudomotivations:

Money, health, and safety are examples of things that seem like motivations, but are not. Objects, categories, and hard-to-define ideas can all be pseudomotivations.

Compensation:

People are not stupid, and they will try to compensate for their weaknesses. By recognizing compensation a persuader gains a valuable tool. People are also unable to judge themselves, because they want gains to be true and losses to be false.

Self-Delusion:

It is very difficult for people to evaluate themselves, and we usually do so in a way that is over-complimentary. Similarly, to avoid manipulation we must avoid falling prey to our own motivations.

Now that the two preparation steps are complete, we are ready to being actively persuading in *Step 3: Open & Disarm.*

STEP
· 03

Open & Disarm

Start a conversation and remove all concerns.

TAKE A DEEP BREATH.

YOU'RE ABOUT TO MEET A STRANGER.

First impressions are bullshit.

Don't believe the hype. When persuading, we will often have to start a conversation with someone we have never met before – a stranger – but a first impression isn't nearly as important as you might think it is.

Persuading a friend often gives us the luxury of almost-instant rapport, but when it involves a person we have no experience with, Step 3 becomes much more important.

We have all been forced into situations, whether socially or professionally, that require conversations with new people. Cocktail parties where we have to mingle with potential clients or friends of a spouse, meetings with busy contractors or babysitters, or hard-to-get job interviews are typical first encounters of the persuasive kind.

First encounters can come in a variety of unexpected flavors as well, like being a talk show guest and making an impression on a television audience, or a class reunion where we have to re-meet people we once knew, or even meeting your significant other's family for the first time.

For many people, including myself, approaching a stranger or meeting a person you have never met can induce a natural social fear. We immediately feel apprehensive, but this is a built-in feeling, especially when approaching someone attractive or important. It's called *approach anxiety* and it's normal! In fact, the person you're approaching feels it too, and if we fix it for them, they will fix it for us automatically.

One of psychology's most-abused statistics is about first impressions. Everybody has probably heard that we (especially women) tend to decide within 15 seconds whether we like someone or not. "You never get a second chance, to make a first impression." This is true, and irrelevant in real life. Advertising and popular culture have turned a "first impression" into a social holy grail, when in truth it's just the first 15 seconds. Of course you're deciding whether you like someone or not! What else would you do during that 15 seconds?

The two real questions we should be asking are:

1. How *should* we use those first 15 seconds?
2. How does it affect the rest of the interaction?

The major problem with a lot of "pop-psychologists" is that they forget that people aren't idiots (well, most people anyway). Think about it: if you met someone new and they spent their first 15 seconds making a bad joke or being nervous, and then turned out to be a fantastic person, are you really going to stick to your first impression? I wouldn't. Sometimes the first 15 seconds are someone else introducing you, so if you can smile and shake a hand, you're set! In reality, most people would only have a fleeting memory of that first impression, if any at all.

The best evidence of this is that most people have a problem remembering names of people they have just met. Are we trusting those same people to remember everything else from the first 15 seconds, hours later? Just relax, and remember that the other person feels just like you do. If you break the ice, you'll be fine.

The first question, "How should we use those first 15 seconds?" is one we have covered a lot so far, and the short answer is: value. If we display social value, that first 15 seconds takes care of itself. Relax. Smile. Be confident and positive. Just talk to them like they are your old friend. The easier it is for them, the easier it will be for you.

136

One of the best examples of this sort of calm, confident demeanor is James Bond. He speaks slowly and calmly, sometimes even taking a second to consider his response before saying anything. He gestures firmly and with purpose, not quickly and nervously. He stands with a relaxed, upright posture without leaning into anyone. If anything, he leans back a little, as if he might decide to leave at any moment because they haven't won his interest yet. He is decisive, smart, and honest, and never, ever, appears to give a single thought to potentially embarrassing himself. He only speaks when he can contribute to the conversation, and otherwise he enjoys listening. And, something you may not have noticed is that he generally doesn't try to detract from anyone else. He assumes he is liked, he assumes he is attractive, and vôila! It comes true.

The equivalent behavior for a woman might be exemplified – perhaps controversially – by someone like Carla Bruni-Sarkozy, former supermodel, artist, former girlfriend of Eric Clapton and Mick Jagger, and current First Lady of France. She, like Bond, manages to mix sexuality and elegance with intelligence and social confidence. She speaks calmy, downplays her public image while maintaining it well, and seems incredibly down-to-earth. She even played acoustic guitar during an interview with Barbara Walters!

I am not saying you have to start wearing a tuxedo and ordering your martini "shaken, not stirred." But whether you are a man or a woman you can appreciate the seductive appeal of a James Bond or Carla Bruni-Sarkozy self-presentation. Everyone either wants to be them, or be with them.

The second question, "how does it affect the rest of the interaction?" will give you some comfort if you worry about meeting new people. The first impression has no impact on the rest of the interaction whatsoever. None. *If you act with value*, the first 15 seconds vanish into many minutes of successful conversation. If you make an ass of yourself and then act with value, they still vanish! If you act like a jerk and continue to be a jerk, that's when you have problems, because, well... you're a jerk.

Pick up artists (PUA's) often say something insulting during their 'opener' just to kick-start the conversation and then spend the next minute or so building it into a flirt. Interrogators have it even worse: they have to arrest someone and then proceed to gain their trust while moving toward a confession. One of the basics of stand-up comedy is to address any physical oddities about yourself before proceeding with your act. A little awkward, perhaps, but it takes care of that nagging detail for the rest of the conversation. And even boring business meetings can have hiccups as everyone gets acquainted.

So if a first impression isn't a big deal, why is this a Universal Step of Persuasion at all? Because persuaders don't worry about first impressions, they focus on starting conversations. And for a lot of people this is the most stressful part. Having a mental floor plan of a persuasion has to include your entry point, and some examples never hurt. "Opening" even has clichés of it's own, like "always start a speech with a joke". A good conversational opening is just social lubricant; it makes your life (and their life!) easier.

In this step we will learn three concepts that create a masterful opening: creating interest, disarming concerns, and indifference. Forget your "first impression" and focus on starting a conversation!

CREATING INTEREST

There were many of the persuasive disciplines that included an attention-getter element at the very beginning. For copywriters it is part of AIDA(S), the oldest copywriting formula around. Hollywood movies and television shows typically begin with a dramatic or exhilarating opening scene that piques our interest. The most important part of a website is the "home" page, because that is where people decide if the site is "good" or not.

I once read an example of this concept being misused by a student in her university term paper. She had learned that getting the reader's attention was important, therefore her first sentence was "F*CK

YOU!". Her professor was not amused.

So, a word of warning as we discuss this idea: set aside a second or two to decide which will serve you better: "interest" or "shock and awe".

Of all the disciplines researched for this book, PUA's easily took the cake when it came to 'opening' with a stranger or group of strangers. When the goal is to pick up a beautiful girl in a bar (who has probably been approached by several guys already), you have to be original and engaging and confident. PUA's expend a great deal of effort studying, sharing, and trying opening lines. In most persuasions the start of the conversation has much lower pressure and expectations, but it's always good to learn from the best.

Beginner PUA's are taught to begin with an insult, which they call a "neg". The goal is not to hurt the girl's feelings, but instead to give guys with less-than-ideal charm skills an entry point that creates an advantage. A question like "is your hair real?" isn't completely insulting and it establishes a certain, je ne sais quoi. The girl, who is used to always being in control, is no longer the most valuable one. While she is deciding whether he is a jerk or not, he charms her friend with a compliment. Those mixed signals create immediate interest and the PUA's value is left intact. If he has executed this well, the first girl might even be jealous of her friend. And it all started with a questionable first impression!

This strategy is not recommended for all scenarios. Indeed, it has been cultivated specifically for picking up girls who have heard it all. What it does demonstrate quite well is that a first impression need not be good at all, and it is much more important for the other person to get into the conversation "for real" whether positively or negatively.

Experienced PUA's – to drive home my point – leave the negging behind and just start the conversation, because their impenetrable self-confidence is intriguing enough to create interest. A PUA master (or self-styled "dating coach") by the alias of "Cajun" was once featured on a reality show called Keys to the VIP. He was, indeed, a master. I couldn't haved described his method better than one of the hosts, who referred to Cajun's confidence as "legendary".

Throughout this step I will assume you are mingling at a cocktail party or social event or a public place, or something like that. During arranged meetings or in a business context introductions are usually expected, so it's not nearly as difficult to get things moving. The key is *not* to treat this like a script; that is a weakness of the pick-up strategy. Go with the flow and smile!

The 14 core motivations we learned in Step 2 are going to be useful throughout our persuasions, starting now.

I used to have a habit — after a drink or four — of sitting down at other people's tables and saying hi, and I have never once been scorned. Especially at formal events. On one particular occassion at a table of 13 people they revealed later that everyone assumed I knew someone else at the table. If you've taken someone's chair or if the conversation isn't fun, just thank them and move on! You will forever be the charming person who came over to say hello. From time to time you will end up with a whole new group of friends.

Done with confidence, saying "hi" can be the best and simplest way to begin a conversation, and I highly recommend it. However, if you seem to have a reason for speaking to this person, that helps. It can be as simple as "Hi, I am trying to meet everyone here tonight, and who might you be?"

The first thing you say should be something that encourages talking. "Open" questions that don't have a yes/no answer are best, especially if they "come out of left field" a bit. Some random examples would be asking where they bought a piece of clothing ("Cool jacket, where did you get it?"), asking for advice or opinions on anything at all ("Excuse me, I am thinking of having dinner somewhere after this, any recommendations?"), accusing them of something trivial with humor ("are you following me?"), casually stating an observation about them ("Wow, you look exactly like my friend Jane."), or, in the case of attraction, even a back-handed compliment can get things started ("Those shoes look really comfortable."). Door-to-door salesmen often look for something in the yard (cars, kids toys, etc.) that indicate a topic of interest. Then they start the conversation with, "Hi, before I tell you why I'm here, can I ask about your basketball hoop?" Instant conversation with a total stranger.

Have you ever noticed how comedians come on stage and just start? They often skip any introduction at all and just get straight to the jokes. Otherwise they will immediately bring the crowd together with comments about the city or the audience or whatever. As it turns out, that works well in real life too. Don't worry too much about social conventions when you start a conversation, just do it. Worst case scenario, introducing yourself is a great thing to do if the conversation goes stale immediately. "Oh, I forgot to introduce myself, I'm YourNameHere. And you are?"

In advertising and copywriting, a general trend is to start with a promise, benefit, or qualifier of some kind. A great example in person is "Hey, wanna see a card trick?" Almost nobody says no to that. You don't have to be a magician to start a conversation though. If you have something else that serves that purpose, use it! Stuff like, "Hey did you know...?" or "How many times a year would you say you rotate your tires?"

PUA's often ask for an opinion: "Hey, let me get your opinion on something. Do you think it's wrong for a guy to take a call from his ex-girlfriend when he is with his new girlfriend?" Opinion-based conversations tend to go for a long time and lead into other topics as well, especially if they are slightly controversial. You should have a reason for asking or offering if possible, even if you're just trying to practice your card tricks or settle a fictitious argument with a friend.

When you imagine some of these in your head they may seem awkward, because you wouldn't normally start conversations with strangers. However, next time you are with your friends, pay attention to how people start conversations or change subjects. Good friends speak mostly in statements rather than questions, and on paper that can seem abrupt. It is very common for one friend to say to another "You're not gonna believe what happened to me at Wal-Mart today..."

141

or something similar. Some stories begin with "Oh my god, it was so funny..." No introduction, no canned lines, no forethought... they just want to tell you a story, so they do.

It works just as well with strangers. I promise.

Anything can start a conversation, and to make an even more persuasive opening we should include a motivational gain for the other person. Something that will make them feel good without sacrificing ourselves. If you approach some strangers with a smile and say "You look like you're up to no good. Whatever it is, I'm in!" you have implied that you want to join their group *(Affiliation)* and that you are not shy *(Status, even if you are shy)*.

Think of the 14 core motivations and how you could start a conversation with them. All people everywhere have those motivations in common, so they are almost no-fail if you give someone a motivational gain in the process.

If there are food or drinks, ask for a recommendation or offer some yourself. I once made a friend at an outdoor festival by offering him an extra beer (I bought one too many for my friends). I said hi, we chatted a bit, and his friends included me in the next 5 rounds! *(Hunger/Thirst/Affiliation)*

Anything that involves kids is usually a just-add-water type of conversation. If there are kids present, ask which ones are theirs. If they have some, say they're cute, they look like they're having fun, ask how old they are, or whatever. If they don't have kids, ask what brings them to this kid-inclusive place. If you don't have kids, ask what it's like, or about anything related to the kid lifestyle ("Is it true that they poo like 5 times a day? Really? You must be better with poo than me."). *(Love, Protection of Kids)*

If couples are present, any questions or comments about them as a couple are good-to-go. "You guys look great together." "So, how did you meet?" "Wow, opposites really do attract!" *(Love for a Mate)*

Find anything in common with anyone. "You look like you're a runner, are you?" "I have the same belt! How great are we?" "I noticed your bumper sticker for Hockey Team ABC, did you see the game yesterday?" *(Affiliation)*

Give someone a chance to name-drop or brag about something. "So who do you know here?" "We were just discussing celebrities we have met, got any good ones?" "You seem interesting, who are you?" *(Status)*

Justice is a challenge sometimes, but in the right context it can be fantastic, because people usually have strong opinions about what is "right". An email went around my office (and the internet) once about a homeless man with an excellent radio voice, and the reason that it was such a fascinating story was that such a talent "deserves" recognition. Those kinds of stories make great "Hey did you hear about..." openers. Or, if you happen to be at an event or among company that have an interest in common, like a charity or vegetarians or environmental activists, you're golden. Whether you are for, or against their position, it's a conversation.

Many of the previous examples were also built on curiosity. If someone "won't believe what happened at Wal-Mart" they are probably already curious. The classic example is starting a story with "Did you hear about Mohammed? Oh, no I wasn't supposed to tell..." *(Status, Curiosity)*

At events where people form small groups (i.e. – most events), it really is as easy as stepping into a group unannounced and saying hi. It creates immediate curiosity, and if you seem friendly people will usually give you a chance to jump in.

There are a million different things you can say to start a conversation, and it doesn't have to be especially clever. Our goal in this step is just to be talking and have the other person talk back. About anything. I read about one guy approaching another guy on the street to ask how he trims his unibrow so well, and they became friends. Starting a conversation through online dating websites can be as simple as asking a nonsense question like "What is your favorite kind of ice cream?" Most people are at least curious enough to ask why you're asking.

DISARM CONCERN

It is always important to look at both sides of any situation. We may have anxiety about approaching strangers, but they also have anxiety about being approached. So we have to immediately disarm the general concerns they might have about us.

People will be put at ease when they get the answers to three questions:

1. Are you scary or weird?
2. Why are you talking to them?
3. When are you leaving?

That might seem cold, but remember, this is their internal dialogue. They would think that about any person that approached and so would you. If they're having anxiety about being approached it will be about one of those things.

First of all, how you physically approach someone can matter. Regardless of gender it is safest to approach someone at an angle so they can see you coming but don't feel confronted.

If you're a man, never approach other men directly from the front, it can seem confrontational. Even turning your own body slightly as if you're going to join their pace makes it seem more co-operative. Avoid approaching a woman from the back, (it feels like you're sneaking up on them) or if you must, a hand on their shoulder can be a gentle warning that you're there.

If you're a woman no one will feel threatened by you, physically, but a man may be intimidated that you're approaching at all. In terms of physical approaches, women have an advantage that way. As long as you don't seem angry or upset, you'll be fine. No persuasion should ever include anger or defensiveness.

Seating arrangements can have an effect as well and we will learn more about that in Step 4.

Remember Step 1, where we learned about valuable behaviour.

WORRY OFTEN GIVES A SMALL THING A BIG SHADOW.

SWEDISH PROVERB

You can eliminate the first concern just by being friendly. If you're not scary or weird, they will see that; there is no reason to mention it. If you don't intend to do anything bad to them (and you shouldn't) then there is nothing to be nervous about either. By talking to them like a friend, they will become a friend.

Having a reason – even a simple one – will disarm the second concern. All of the conversational openers above included some kind of purpose. The key thing to realize is that the reason you want to start the conversation is not the same as your ultimate purpose for talking to them sometimes. If you have approached this stranger to sell them something, do not start with "Hi, I am selling this thing..." because you're dead in the water. In persuasion we rarely state our intentions from the outset (only formal competitive debating seems to do that, because they have to.) Door-to-door 'coupon salesmen' who are selling 2-for-1 coupons for pizza start with "Hi! We are coming around the neighbourhood today to ask one quick question: how many pizzas do you eat in a month?" The answer, of course, reveals how many coupons you should buy.

The third concern is about setting a time limit. The PUA version goes something like "Hi, I have to get back to my friends in a second, but I just wanted to ask your opinion on something..." The cocktail party version might be more like "Hi everybody, I'm _____, Jim's business partner. I'm just circulating to meet everyone for a minute... so, how do you know Jim?" The business meeting version might take a more serious tone, but have the same effect, "Thanks for coming everyone. I'm _____, the Regional Marketing Director for Company B. I have another meeting at 2 o'clock, so I'd like to wrap up here in 45 minutes or so, if no one objects."

Movies and television have to show us immediately what they are all about, otherwise we get fidgety. If the goal of a movie doesn't start to shine through after 10 or 20 minutes, it's boring. If a comedian's joke doesn't seem to go anywhere it starts losing it's humour. If you don't understand why you're learning something in school, it's boring. Give people context, and they will quickly settle into it.

Comedians, movies, television shows, school classes, etc. typically have a time limit and everyone knows it.

You get the idea. The goal is to make everyone feel comfortable with the situation before they have a chance to feel uncomfortable, and all that takes is a bit of information. What we say during the first minute of conversation doesn't even have to be remotely true to effectively start a conversation, it just has to disarm those immediate concerns. You may stay and have drinks with a woman for hours. You may find a lot in common with people at the park and chat for a while. And when was the last time a business meeting ended on time? If things go well, everyone will be happy to continue talking. If not, you're happy to have met them, and you can move along as planned.

In certain situations there may be other concerns that should be fixed immediately, like trustworthiness. A fourth concern that you may feel the need to disarm is "Can I trust this person?" Put yourself in the other person's shoes. If there is any reason to doubt your intentions, disarm those concerns too. You know your intentions but they don't. A manipulator would pay particular attention to disarming this concern, because their intentions are bad, so don't over-do it.

Real trust is something that is built through rapport, and real trust is hard to build in the first minute. You can offer a small gesture of good will to disarm the "fear" that you have approached with manipulative intentions.

The bed salesman that says "Don't buy that one, it's over priced. This one over here is just as good and I have it at home" has created trust and pitched a product all in one smooth motion. With a skeptical customer that can make a huge difference.

We must be careful not to overwhelm ourselves with "potential" concerns, because it only leads to disarming concerns that don't actually exist. A person that is constantly trying to solve problems before they exist seems needy, insecure, and fearful. Just relax.

The Greenpeace kids that fund-raise on the street almost always come at you, flashing their green binders, looking like they're trying to capture you before you escape. And people avoid them accordingly.

The fund-raisers may feel that the binder displays value, because to them it represents something they are proud of. For the rest of us it displays their intention to ask us for money.

In addition, their typical greeting is something like: "Excuse me sir, we're collecting donations for Greenpeace..." and by that time most people have walked past them with their heads down.

If they approached with more value they would get a long way with an opener like: "Hi! We're just asking everybody a one-question survey: How can we get more people to use eco-friendly lightbulbs?" (the question doesn't matter, as long as it is easy and relevant) This disarms all immediate concerns: a reason for approaching (and a reason for having a clipboard), a short time frame (one-question only), and it's friendly (Hi!). And it says nothing about money.

One final note about creating interest is that we shouldn't underestimate the details or environmental factors. Car dealers often display their high-end automobiles at the airport because executive business travellers are there so frequently. The display itself is usually brightly lit and includes the car itself, in the middle of the airport. If that weren't enough, attractive women often stand with the car, handing out magazine-style brochures. These women are not typically hired for their astute automotive insights, needless to say.

Since executives interested in flashy cars are more likely to be men, this is a winner. Whether they are interested in the car, the women, the brochure, or whether they just want to kill 10 minutes looking at something shiny, the entire scenario makes it easy to succumb to the "conversation" between the traveller and the car dealership.

INDIFFERENCE

Valuable behaviour is obviously a large part of persuasion, and *indifference* is a large part of valuable behaviour. It has been mentioned several times so far, but this step and the next step are when the true value of indifference is maximized.

Imagine you see a few pennies on the sidewalk as you walk by. Do you stop to pick them up? Maybe, maybe not. You are indifferent. You have lots of pennies; why are these ones so special? If someone offered those pennies as a reward for an unpleasant task, you would probably just say no. It wouldn't be bad to have those pennies, and you'll take them if it isn't too much trouble, but if someone puts a significant obstacle between you and the pennies, it isn't worth it. Similarly, if something you want costs a few pennies, the cost isn't really a factor in your decision-making. You are *indifferent* about paying it.

If you are extremely poor, that cost would matter quite a lot more.

Now imagine a similar scenario in which you are a person hiring a new employee. 500 people apply for your job and they are all great. Then one excellent candidate says he will only take the job if you offer a higher salary. You would be indifferent, because there are 499 other excellent candidates perfectly happy with the lower salary.

If you only had one excellent application and he asked for a higher salary, you would be much more likely to accommodate that request, rather than hiring no one.

That is indifference. The amount of attention you give to each and every thing all day long indicates its value to you — right here, right now — including people. If you have 10,000 spoons, another spoon is not worth a lot to you, but a knife is very valuable. Don'tcha think?

You are not arrogant, or elitist, and you still think it might be a good thing to have a particularly nice spoon, but in the end, you're just not that concerned. You will also not get angry if you lose a spoon, and honestly, you might not even notice. You are not threatened if someone else gets it first. Actually, you might be happy for them! They're on their way to a fine spoon collection like yours!

Indifference is a surprisingly powerful tactic in sales, attraction, interrogation, politics, and almost any situation where social value makes a difference. Everyone else assumes that if you are indifferent, you must encounter this situation regularly.

Imagine you are applying for the job now, and the job is the same as the one you already have. You wouldn't be particularly intimidated by the interview because you already have a job like this. You are happy to do the interview and discuss your qualifications, but you don't need this job, so there is no fear of rejection, no extra effort to please the interviewer, and you are fairly sure you'll get the job, given your over-qualification. And if you don't, that's ok too, and you can wish them luck in their search for the right person. You are indifferent.

Now imagine the same situation, but instead of a job it is an attractive woman at a bar, and although she is beautiful, you have had many beautiful girlfriends. You walk up and say hello, and get a luke-warm response. You are indifferent, so you're not concerned about succeeding or failing. The fact that you approached her in the first place was sheerly out of curiosity, so you might continue to push through the attitude, laughing occasionally at her playing hard to get.

This works on men to some degree as well, but is particularly powerful on attractive women.

"Real" indifference in people is created by *adverse selection*. Any situation where many people are competing for someone or something, creates adverse selection. When 10 guys all want an attractive woman, or when 500 applicants apply for a single job, that is adverse selection. The person in control of that resource is indifferent: they feel no regret about the people or things that are not chosen, and the person or thing that is chosen will be the most valuable, of course. Adverse selection is the best scenario for the chooser, because they can't lose. If you can't lose, you become indifferent, because you're merely choosing how to win. We should all be so lucky.

The good news is that you can act indifferently, even when it is a special opportunity, to increase your chances of persuasive success.

The people who want the woman or the job the most are the people that will gain the most by being chosen *(Sex, Status)*.

This applies to all core motivations: the bigger the gain, the more effort it is worth. If it would be a huge promotion, you will work as hard as you can to win the position. If you have never been with a woman as attractive as this one, you might do everything you can to impress her. In both cases, you will not be chosen, because you are the least qualified candidate. Your effort (and probably your competence) proves it. The best strategy against an adverse situation is indifference. The fewer options available for the other person, the more actively you can pursue your goal.

This is why an attractive person is most attracted to someone who plays hard-to-get, an unattractive person is attracted to anyone who gives them attention, and a billionaire tends to concern themselves with things that are one-of-a-kind or money-can't-buy experiences.

It is quite counter-intuitive at first, and in persuasion it is one of your biggest behavioural advantages.

This is the attitude of a socially valuable person, all the time. With men or women, friends or strangers, and any opportunity, big or small, indifference can make you the most socially valuable person in the room.

Indifference is a very challenging technique to master. If you can, you will immediately see results. When approaching someone new, indifference can seem to have almost magical powers, especially in attraction, and can be completely irresistible in a lot of persuasive situations.

When you approach a stranger to start a conversation, consider how a person who approaches strangers often would act in that situation. PUA's approach 10, 20, or 50 women in a night when they are beginners, just for the practice. Door-to-door salesmen ring up to 100 doorbells per day. Eventually, it starts to become routine, and real indifference settles in. Ironically, when you stop focusing on succeeding, success rates start to increase.

Be indifferent during the first 15 seconds of your conversation and it will send the message that you have high social value, and the other person will instantly feel comfortable with you.

AVOID MANIPULATION

Throughout this book we will discuss ways to avoid being manipulated wherever possible. In this case, however, I feel it would be irresponsible to suggest skepticism when someone approaches you. Regardless of your gut feelings or first impressions, a person can turn out to be the opposite of what they seemed to be, or precisely what they seemed to be. Either way, only time will tell.

If someone approaches and gives you the "scary and weird" vibe, don't wait around to find out. You might just misunderstand them or they could also be about to rob you. Err on the side of caution if you feel genuinely uncomfortable.

If a person seems overly-focused on disarming a particular concern, or a concern you hadn't even considered, take note of it, because it means that in their mind, that should be a concern. People often focus most on their own weaknesses (in their own opinion).

If you are buying a house, watch for where the real estate agent looks, but doesn't mention. If they seem like they are trying to convince you that a particular feature or room is very useful, they might be compensating because they actually see it as a weak point. If it were actually useful, they would assume you think so too.

If someone spontaneously approaches you and they are friendly and engaging, have a chat! During your conversation, keep in mind that they may have a bigger motive in mind. It doesn't mean the bigger motive is bad, it should just be a matter of interest. If, 10 minutes later, they bring up something you should buy from them, or a reason you should give them something... raise the red flag. If they offer great conversation and then say goodnight or ask for your contact details, consider agreeing!

TRY THIS AT HOME

Starting a conversation is easy, and it's even easier when the other person can't go anywhere. Choose someone in a service position, like the cashier at a grocery store or a cab driver. Start a conversation with them about anything and make it last longer than a typical transaction.

Focus on putting the other person at ease as soon as you can. Let them know you don't intend to take their entire day to talk. Have a simple reason why you are asking them, and try to make it a compliment for them: "You seem like a stylish person. Which fashion magazine do you like best? My sister asked me to pick one up for her, but I don't know what to choose…" And be indifferent! They are just a random person working at the register; you have nothing to lose.

Anyone can make idle chit-chat while you go through the checkout; this should be a conversation about something you have chosen and initiated, and it should disrupt their normal routine, in a good way.

For example, if you get a cab, find out where the driver worked before being a taxi driver, and why they chose to become a driver. Don't ask if it has been busy today. Cab drivers often see and know a lot of stuff about the city they drive in; ask questions!

Bonus points if you can do it with someone from a different culture.

SUMMARY

First impressions are bullshit. Don't believe the hype. What you do in the first 15 seconds has little-to-no effect on the outcome of your persuasion.

To start a conversation and make a strong first impression you must do three things when you approach: create interest, disarm concerns, and be indifferent.

Open:
Opening with motivation means engaging the other person with a comment or question that is relevant to them and achieves a gain in one of the 14 motivations.

Disarm concerns:

Disarming concerns is done to create comfort. We must let them know who we are, why we have said hello, and what time frame this conversation is meant to take (shorter is better). This does not have to be true or accurate; the goal is the comfort of the other person.

Indifference:

Indifference is the art of behaving like you do this every day, or more, and therefore you are not really concerned with the outcome. You are social, confident, and patient, and never impulsive or needy. We don't say we're indifferent; we show it. If you choose to let them have you, lucky them. If not, on to the next great opportunity.

In Step 4 we will learn to make someone need you, like you, and want you. This will include creating the perception of a need using the 14 core motivations, and gaining trust. Then we will turn the persuasion around so the other person convinces us that we should be the solution to their need.

STEP
04

Create Rapport & Needs

Make them like you, need you, and want you.

IF YOU'RE LOOKING FOR THE "SECRET" OF PERSUASION, THIS IS IT.

Rapport (Rah-POR):

When people are genuinely getting along, with feelings of mutual enjoyment, trust, and communication. Without rapport persuasion gets very difficult. With excellent rapport, persuasion sometimes solves itself.

When it comes to rapport, it will take as long as it has to. Relax and be patient. If you are too eager to move onto later steps and sacrifice rapport to get there, you are only hurting yourself. Patience not only ensures that you're doing this step correctly, it is also a key ingredient in valuable behaviour.

In long persuasions you may need days or weeks for Step 4 to get the other person properly motivated toward your goal.

It is also important to point out that this step may have to highlight the persuader's good reputation if it isn't known by the person being persuaded. Whether it is an expert being introduced as an expert, or the persuader mentioning the awards and degrees, or just valuable behavior that silently proves the persuader's confidence, the other person must understand that this is a person worth listening to. If the persuader's reputation has been undermined by someone else already, rapport will be difficult to create until that problem has been solved.

In this chapter we will assume that the persuader's reputation is intact. If it isn't intact, the best method is to give examples that establish credibility and/or find a person that is trusted by the person being persuaded to "vouch" for the persuader.

Step 4 is a three-part process, where all three parts happen almost at the same time. It can require concentration to keep track of, but when done properly it is the most elegant and effective aspect of persuasion.

The three parts are:

1. Make Them Like You
2. Make Them Need You
3. Make Them Want You

In that order.

People often say "isn't that three steps?" when they learn about this, but it is important to realize that they happen together, and come as a package.

Rapport was the Step that all effective persuaders from any discipline had in common. Interrogators, politicians, PUA's, fortune tellers, cult leaders, comedians, screenplay writers, and on, and on, and on. And they all execute this three-part step in roughly the same way. Psychologists and behavioral economists call a similar idea "priming". It can be done in writing or in person or with images, but it must always be done.

To make us like them, a persuader will use isopraxis and a technique called mirroring, which is used by hypnotists, salespeople, and hostage negotiators to gain trust and form a good relationship out of nothing. Basically, the persuader will become the other person's mirror (socially speaking) on purpose to create a good connection with them.

Politicians use demographics and opinion polls to measure the opinions of their voters, and then choose opinions for themselves that fit the majority of people, in order to secure a maximum number of votes.

Comedians often open a show with jokes and observations about the audience and their town to make them feel as if the comedian relates to them somehow.

Interrogators often empathize with the criminal, and agree that anyone would have done the same in their position. In reality their opinions couldn't be more different.

As I edited this chapter, a 60-Minutes interview was on television, with an American interrogator named Ali Soufan, who interrogated Al-Qaeda members after the 9-11 attack. He said that rapport was crucial with the terrorists, because if the interrogators were disrespectful, it justified the hateful image of Americans that Al-Qaeda are taught.

However, if the terrorists were offered coffee or tea, and spoken to like intelligent people (which they were), it disagreed with that image, and the terrorists let down their guard. Even with enemies, rapport is very important.

To make someone need us, we must create a need in general. By using the 14 core motivations the persuader will identify one or more motivations that are of interest to the other person, and emphasize. A persuader can also create a need by making the other person perceive a core motivation in a new way.

Advertising and news stories often use sensationalism to create needs. The Swine Flu was publicized as a global epidemic and a serious threat to your life, even though the actual Swine Flu death rate was less than the normal flu in any given year. The result was a shortage of Swine Flu vaccines even though doctors often have trouble motivating people to get normal flu shots in any other year.

When a fortune-teller begins to tell your fortune they typically navigate through vague concerns common to everyone, like health, wealth and relationships. Some clients even tell the psychic precisely what they want to know about, and it's all good news and miraculous insights after that.

To make someone want us we will use the needs and the friendship we have built to begin leading the other person. Instead of mirroring and following their lead, we will begin to make them qualify for *our* agreement. This effectively turns the persuasion around so that instead of us trying to talk them into an agreement, we become the solution they are trying to earn. Basically, it's a bait and switch, and all good persuaders do it, whether they realize it or not.

The interrogator who was empathetic 5 minutes ago is now asking for information or a confession so he has the ability to get the criminal a deal. Even though it sounds like the interrogator is trying to help the criminal, it is the criminal who has to qualify to be helped.

The fortune-teller will provide a vague piece of information like a name or an address, and then make the client provide the meaning. "I'm seeing a name that starts with A, and a yellow house. Does that make sense to you?" The client then searches their mind and suggests "Maybe it's my friend Jane's yellow house?" The fortune teller creates a good fit, "Yes! It was the sound of A in "Jane" that I heard; it is her house!" The client then leaves believing the psychic knew about Jane and her yellow house, when it was actually the client that provided the information.

Screenplay writers make us like the characters and then give the characters a problem to solve, at which point we, the audience, are on the edge of our seats waiting to see how the story unfolds. While the characters began by demonstrating the good traits they share with us, now it is we who are following them.

An infomercial, in a somewhat more transparent manner, connects your supposed "need" to a new product that solves this need like never before! The host's enthusiastic sympathy for your pain has now shifted to a demonstration of how easy it is to solve that pain, and it's so cheap! But wait! That's not all...!

In the complete sequence of the 8 Universal Steps, Step 4 creates a crucial point on which the rest of the persuasion balances. Without rapport, the person being persuaded may never fully trust the persuader, and without "benefit of the doubt" a persuasion becomes an uphill climb.

Without a need there is no persuasion. There must always be a motivation for the other person to agree or a benefit for the other person in a persuasion. As they say in advertising: don't sell features, sell benefits. Otherwise, the other person may not even be interested long enough to hear our persuasion in the first place. Regardless of whether they want to help because they are our new friend *(Affiliation)*, or because they stand to gain something special *(Status)*, or because they feel that you deserve it *(Justice)*, there must be a need.

And if a persuader can hit a home run on the turn-around and make the other person fully commit to qualifying themselves, the result will be a willing and eager person, waiting to be convinced (Step 6).

MAKE THEM LIKE YOU

Some people just seem easier to like than others, don't they? It can seem like one of those qualities that we are either born with or not, but be assured that anyone can have that mass appeal if they know what they're doing.

Making someone like you is a universal effect called *Isopraxis*. You may recall that when using Affiliation we look for people like ourselves with whom to become friends. The closer someone is to ourselves (socially) the more we immediately "click." So in theory, everyone would be best friends with their clone, if they could. We want our kids to be like us, we often choose pets that resemble us, we hire people that are like us, and we want to date people who "have a lot in common" with us.

This is exactly why we use a technique called mirroring to mimic the way people talk, stand, sit, gesture, act and think.

Any time two people have rapport with one another they will unconsciously mimic each other's posture and behavior. You can observe this is any public place where people are likely to have long conversations. A café or restaurant is perfect. Look around and you will see a couple with one elbow on the table resting their chins in their hands. You will see two people leaning back. You will see a new couple on a date both leaning forward with both hands together. You will see people take a drink at the same time, especially in groups. None of those people are consciously aware they're doing it, but by doing it they create better rapport.

All people do this when we get along with each other, and if we do it on purpose it is both unnoticeable and looks completely natural. Like many of the techniques in persuasion, mirroring (creating isopraxis on purpose) is something we do anyway. We just usually don't notice.

It is important to note that mirroring is *not imitating*. If you copy someone directly you will look like a fool and they will notice. The idea is to copy the tone of their body language. We're trying to be like them, not to be them. If someone is sitting and we're standing, it is better to crouch to speak with them. If a person leans forward or back move forward or back. When we eat we almost have to mirror them because eating requires a certain set of motions and postures. If someone has one hand on the table, you could put your opposite hand in a similar position (it is called "matching" when you do the same position but not as a mirror image).

Generally when we mirror another person we want it to be subtle. If they change posture slowly, wait 10 seconds before you change to mirror them. It's a completely natural thing to do, and it subconsciously makes them feel like you are "in tune" with them. If the conversation is excited and enthusiastic and someone changes position we can follow them more quickly, since the tone of the conversation is quick and urgent.

The best way to learn mirroring is to watch two people from a distance as they naturally mirror each other.

When two people have rapport, they will face each other more and the distance between their bodies will decrease. Not only will we stand closer, we will actually lean toward each other out of interest. This is particularly noticeable when people are standing or physically attracted to each other. Our feet will often point toward the current

MAKE THEM LIKE YOU

person of interest as well, or – if we don't have rapport – our feet may point toward an exit.

Body language can be "open" or "closed". Open body language includes things like big arm gestures with palms facing the other person, legs uncrossed, and exposing your neck and wrists. You trust the other person so you're not "protecting" yourself or creating physical barriers.

Closed body language is the opposite. Crossed arms and legs, turning away from the other person, tighter arm gestures and hand gestures that hide the palms and wrists, and generally trying to put things between ourselves and the other person like hair, jackets, or objects.

Open body language is ideal during rapport. The more open the better, but don't get discouraged if the other person isn't as open as you would like. They might just be cold.

Body language works both ways: if you feel more open your body will be more open, but if your body is more open, you will also become more open. So if someone isn't showing open body language, open them up! To uncross someone's arms you can give them a drink or a business card to hold, or even an object to play with mindlessly (like a pen). You may be able to ask them to demonstrate the size or shape of an object with their hands, or point to something that is hard to find. If someone doesn't have the body language we want, we can create it through simple, natural conversational requests.

Mirroring and "pacing" are two concepts from Neuro-Linguistic Programming that are also used in a variety of situations like business, sales, and negotiation (hostage and otherwise). If we just want to get into the other person's social context, mirroring is all that is necessary. However, if the other person is in a mood or a frame of mind that is counter-productive – like anger, sadness, or a pessimistic mood – we should "pace" them before we try to change their mood.

Pacing is when you match the other person just before you begin shifting them into a more productive state. Think of a relay runner trying to pass the baton. The next runner starts running to match the pace before they have the baton so the pass is smooth and fluid. When trying to change someone's mind or mood it is advantageous to get into their head space first. Women do this more intuitively than men, but anyone can do it.

The easiest way to pace is through body language. Negative emotions and moods create closed body language. If we mirror that negative body language at first we actually begin to create some positive effects, because we are creating a gain *(Affiliation)*. A sense of belonging and friendship.

If a person is in a negative frame of mind we might begin by agreeing with something they have said, or by conceding a good point they have made. They begin to relax because you are not providing resistance. When someone is sad we sympathize before we try to cheer them up. Once we are on the same team, we can begin to lead them to greener pastures. That is pacing, and it is one of the advantages of mirroring.

By mirroring body language, tonality, and frame of mind with someone who is having a negative experience, we actually make their entire experience more positive, which easily leads to more open body language, a more positive mood, and more suggestibility. When combined with a little validation, everything can get pretty sunny, pretty fast.

Our environment can provide significant assistance or significant barriers to rapport, depending on where we are and what our goals are. For example, imagine a table and you must choose where to sit. You are in the room with one colleague and one potential client. Where do you sit?

Sitting directly across from someone encourages competitive behaviour, because you physically "oppose" each other. Sitting on a corner with the client feels more cooperative because you can both look at things from a similar perspective. And sitting on the same side as the client feels very cooperative, as if you are on the same team.

Imagine a battlefield. If I stand on the other side, am I your enemy or your ally? If I approach from the side, I could be on either side, or I could be a third party in the mix (which is why councellors often sit on neither side). If I stand next to you on the front line, I am clearly fighting for the same goal as you. The same applies with seating arrangements.

If you are forced to sit facing someone else, such as a first date, mirroring becomes particularly effective, and indifference becomes especially important, which we will examine later in this chapter. You can also choose to sit slightly sideways or lean back to ease any tension that is created.

It can also be helpful to adopt the type of language and tone that a person uses. In the same way that you would probably whisper in a church or yell at a baseball game, you can use more big words and complex phrasing with an older professor, and "bad" words and catch phrases with young adults. If someone is loud and gruff, be louder and gruffer. If they are quiet and shy, be more subtle. If someone has low self-esteem, be gentler with their ego. If they are a narcissist play into their self-image.

Emotions are also an excellent thing to mirror. If someone is angry, become louder and more intense (not as much as them) so that you can meet them halfway, and then bring them down.

Ideally you will immerse yourself deeper into their social comfort zone than you might actually be, just because it makes them feel more comfortable. They won't notice that you've changed anything, because when you speak like they speak and act like they act, they think it's normal. For example, if you meet someone who has the same accent as you do you say "Hey! We have the same accent!" or do you think they have no accent? Exactly. Everyone has an accent, but the ones we don't notice are the ones that sound most like us.

CAUTION: If you don't think you can be convincing using another person's style of speaking, don't even try. If they tend to use a lot of technical jargon, or if you are trying to relate to people much younger than you, trying to be like them may only emphasize how different you are. When in doubt, go with a neutral style of talking and avoid any expressions or new euphemisms at all. And be curious about differences, not dismissive or presumptuous. Old advertising executives are notorious for believing they have their finger on the pulse of the youth when they are actually completely out of touch.

Cultural differences are some of the most important and most difficult things to mirror. As much as we might feel like everyone else will love our culture as much as we do, try to resist the temptation to immerse them into it. Instead, learn and do as they do. As Ron Burgundy says, "When in Rome...." Show the other person that you love their culture as much as they do. Cultural differences are only a problem if you make them one.

One of the most irrational emotions we can have is when people get "angry" or "insulted" because a different culture does something differently. It taps directly into our Justice motivation, because Justice, fairness, and "rightness" is related to a particular group, and when someone doesn't act "right" in our group, our first instinct is to think their way is "wrong". It's not wrong. It's different, so try it.

When friends spend a lot of time with each other their expressions, body language, and even style of laughing change to be more similar to each other. Couples in long relationships think, talk, and act similarly. Kids grow up to be like parents, sometimes even in minute details. Isopraxis is a silent, but powerful social force, and persuaders use it to their advantage wherever possible.

If you feel like this might be too manipulative for you, consider the fact that you already do it with all of your closest friends and family, and they do it to you.

THE EXCEPTION TO THE RULE

There is a certain scenario when we want to withold rapport at first, and that is when someone else holds the resources in an *adverse selection* scenario.

What?! Resist the most important step in persuasion?

Yup.

Good rapport is normally supposed to make the persuader and the other person equals, but that is not always a good thing.

In Step 3 it was important to understand how adverse selection creates indifference for the person with control. That person expects everyone to be interested in them or what they have. The people who wouldn't be interested are people who have no need for that resource, or people who are more valuable than that resource.

For example, we looked at the situation where 500 excellent candidates have applied for a single job, so the person hiring is indifferent when one of those people isn't a good match. But now imagine that the job being offered is the cashier spot at McDonald's. A perfectly good job if you're 18 years old, but if it were offered to the CEO of a major corporation, it would be far too little to get his interest. If the CEO was a high-value person she would politely decline and wish them luck in their search as she moves on to her board meeting.

What that CEO would be doing is resisting rapport. She has no negative feelings toward this person, and in a small way it could be a flattering offer, but she is also not going to break her pattern to make a good impression on the representative from McDonald's.

This is the strategy to be used when we are trying to persuade someone and the other person has all the control. When we resist rapport – making them work to make us interested – it sends the message that regardless of how many options they have, we are on a whole other level.

Resisting rapport can be a delicate operation. If we actually are interested in getting what they have then we can't kill rapport, but we can't give it away either. So we play a push-and-pull game. This is commonly called "mixed signals" or "playing cat-and-mouse". Give a little, and take a little. "What you have sounds interesting, but what's in it for me?"

A PUA's secret weapon is the fact that an attractive girl assumes the PUA wants to be with her. So when the PUA works against that assumption, the girl no longer has any weapons. "You want to take me home? What's in it for me?" She assumed that going home with her was what was in it for him. Apparently not.

In flirting this is very effective. With a slight change of tonality it can also work in any situation. When interviewing for jobs, set up more than one interview and refuse to "decide" until you have heard from all of the companies. Tell all companies what the others are offering. If 500 applications come in, but only one of them is wanted by all your competitors, suddenly there is only 1 application that matters.

The best way to beat adverse selection and indifference from someone else, is to fight fire with fire. Never be defensive, insulting, angry, competitive, threatened, etc. There is a reason people remember "the one that got away". It's because they got away. Nobody feels that more than someone who used to be indifferent.

When we mirror someone to use isopraxis we temporarily shift the way we behave to be more relatable. We are still ourselves, but we're tailoring how we present ourselves to make the other person feel more at ease. However, we shouldn't do this forever. Once we have gained excellent rapport (which takes time) it is time to test our value in the interaction by leading instead of following. By changing our posture we can test to see if they mirror us unconsciously (Remember, all people do this when they're getting along). If we make a significant shift in our posture or if the other person begins to adopt speech patterns or expressions from us, we know that we have begun to be the valuable one in the exchange.

As the leader we can gradually move someone toward a suggestible frame of mind.

MAKE THEM NEED YOU

Creating a need can be tricky business, but it isn't complicated. There are blunt ways to do it, like infomercials, and cunning ways to do it, like hostage negotiation. It is also possible that a person has a need already, in which case we merely have to recognize and run with it.

Remember that all human needs fall into one of the 14 core motivations. A need is therefore either a potential gain in one of those motivations, or the risk of losing something in one of those motivations. All motivations are also relative, which means that if someone suddenly feels like they don't have enough, or most people have more, it can become a need.

The social motivations are particularly powerful because whether someone is gaining or losing love, affiliation, status, or justice, we're talking about things that are part of our values, beliefs, families, and identities. As someone who moved to a different continent spontaneously I can tell you that you probably underestimate how much those things matter until they change.

There are two simple steps when a persuader creates a need:

1. Select one or more core motivations that are interesting to the other person. (Some conversation might be necessary to figure out what is most relevant.)

2. Emphasize the other person's lack or risk within that motivation. (Try *not* to rub their face in it. Think of something you are genuinely insecure about, and how little it would take to make it an issue.)

If a persuader merely wants someone to try a new food or drink *(hunger & thirst)*, we can wait until they are hungry, or we can tell them about how delicious it is, to make them hungry. Images and sounds about the food or drink – as we discussed in Step 2 – can create that need from scratch without a lot of effort.

Advertising is famous for creating needs that didn't exist before. One of the best quotes from Mad Men is "What you call 'love' was invented by guys like me." Love is a feeling, of course, but what that quote refers to is what we associate with love, like diamond engagement rings, flowers and chocolates on Valentine's Day, and so on.

In a movie about a bank heist, it helps if the characters are forced into a situation where they *need* to rob the bank or they face a greater threat, like an angry mob boss.

Religion tends to use pre-existing needs to entice their congregation to be persuaded. Death, health problems, sex & conception, loss of a loved one, hopes for your children, loneliness, acceptance, success, fairness and redemption, and forgiveness for guilt are all things that the church seems to have influence over via prayers. Interestingly, they all happen to be core motivations too. Once the church has set up the expectation that God can solve all of the things you worry about most, the church merely has to exist, and wait for people to walk in.

The discipline that gains a lot from the effective creation of a need (as opposed to using one that exists) is criminal interrogation. In an interrogation the officers make the rules and control the emotions, so they can work a criminal into a panic over what might happen to them, in order to get confessions or information.

Imagine two criminals have committed a crime, are arrested and brought in for interrogation. The only way the police can get a conviction is if one or both of the criminals confess. They are put in separate rooms and interrogated separately.

The motivations toward friendship *(Affiliation)* and freedom *(Status)* and loyalty *(Justice and Affiliation)* create a scenario where the police are on the outside, looking in. The criminals are more likely to cooperate and save each other than to support the objectives of the police. An interrogator must change the situation so those motivations are a risk instead of a gain. He must create a need he can use for persuasion.

In Game Theory this is called the Prisoner's Dilemma. Here are the rules:

1. If both stay silent, both get a slap on the wrist.

2. If both confess, both get 5 years in jail.

3. If one confesses and one stays silent, the confessor goes free and the silent one gets the death penalty.

Now each criminal must choose between his motivations for Affiliation and Justice, or the motivation for Status and Avoiding Death (maybe the strongest of all motivations). If he chooses to be loyal, and his friend doesn't, that is the worst case scenario. Suddenly loyalty is a risk instead of a gain. The "safest" choice is to confess, because he will get 5 years as a maximum, and freedom as a minimum.

If both criminals are experts in Game Theory they would still cooperate and get a slap on the wrist, because although it is not the "safest", it is the smartest choice. If they were expert persuaders they would realize that an interrogator would only offer this type of deal if they didn't have enough evidence for a conviction.

Intuition fails again.

That was a rather elaborate example, but it doesn't have to be that ingenious. It is no mistake that a lot more food commercials are shown around meal times. PUAs (knowing that attraction is built on value) immediately begin telling stories of their beautiful ex-girlfriends, or displaying competence with magic tricks, games, or humor routines. Hostage Negotiators listen to the criminal's demands or ask questions to assess the motivation for holding the hostages in the first place. Movies present the hero with a dilemma to solve. Military recruiters offer money and respect to young adults who have trouble choosing a path in life.

A need can be a potential gain, or a potential loss, but one way or another we must create a motivational problem to be solved. This is when it becomes important to understand how core motivations work, because we may be presented with a situation, like the Interrogators, where the intrinsic motivations work against us. In that case we need to re-frame those motivations so they become a risk or find another motivation as leverage.

An infomercial about a device (say, a pillow) that alleviates neck pain is only persuasive if you have neck pain. However, if the infomercial implies that you may not be aware of the damage your current pillow is doing to your neck, suddenly no neck pain is a risk. So now neck pain and no neck pain are both warning signs! The only way to be sure you're safe is with this revolutionary pillow, made from space age materials.

The "space age" was decades ago, by the way.

Affiliation and Status motivations can make your perfectly good possessions into substandard possessions in mere moments. Your barbecue has X, Y and Z features and can roast an entire pig at the same time! And until your neighbour gets one that is slightly bigger and has a television built into it, you couldn't be happier. Although it is 100% irrational, the feeling of Status you had moments ago is now replaced with a motivation to "keep up with the Jones'" *(Status)*.

Sometimes motivations can be turned on each other and a person is motivated to do crazy things to avoid a motivational loss. Imagine a rich couple with a prenuptial agreement, and the husband decides to divorce the wife, take the kids, and run off with his secretary. As irrational as it is, we wouldn't have to stretch our imagination too far to see why the wife might think of murdering the husband and framing the secretary. After all, that would save the money and the kids *(Status and Love)*, get rid of the husband and screw over the secretary *(Justice)*. When you understand motivations, it actually starts to make sense.

If we were a hitman, it probably wouldn't take too long to persuade this woman to purchase our services while she can still afford it. If we were an FBI informant, she would be in big trouble.

Without a need, there is no persuasion.

MAKE THEM WANT YOU

Let's review what has been accomplished so far. We have created rapport, which comes with an open atmosphere of trust and friendship.

Then we have deconstructed their perception of needs so they are focused on something they want to get or protect. This provides us an opportunity to re-build what we have deconstructed and to perform the coolest part of any persuasion: the "turn-around".

There are three simple steps when a persuader does a "turn-around":

1. Connect the other person's need to the persuader's ultimate goal.

2. The persuader is then reluctant/unavailable/skeptical/ unprepared to be the solution.

3. The persuader "qualifies" the other person to make them "earn" it.

It can be remarkably easy to connect any random need of someone to a persuader's need. The key is not to make it an instant sales pitch. The objective is to have the other person "realize" the value of the persuader's goal as a way to solve their own need (which has hopefully already been created).

In one way or another the persuasion has to satisfy a need, but since the persuader creates the need, that's not a big problem. Just create a need that is useful.

The counter-intuitive part in Step 4 is when the persuader must act like they are not the solution when they so badly want to be. The reason for this is simple: if, without warning, the persuader jumps on the opportunity to be the solution, it trips a warning signal in the mind of the other person and your carefully-built rapport starts to dissolve before your eyes.

The other person always has to feel like they are making the decision to like you, to be convinced, to agree. As soon as someone is aware they are being persuaded, they will resist just so they don't feel like someone else is controlling them *(Status)*.

So, by being reluctant/unavailable/skeptical/unprepared to be the solution, the persuader avoids that trap, and lets the other person

I AM A MASTER OF THE ART OF FAME.

STEFANI GERMANOTTA
A.K.A. "LADY GAGA"

talk them into it.

The persuader has to make a person "qualify" themselves. Instead of persuading them, they need to prove they are worthy, or "qualified" to have their needs met. This creates an emotional commitment from the other person that makes it feel like they are making a decision rather than being persuaded. And if it comes down to it, the persuader will congratulate them on that decision later.

Have you ever noticed that when you go to the bank for a loan, you have to be qualified to borrow money from them, even though that is how they make profit? Now, it is true that they would make less money if they just lent money to any irresponsible person who walked through the door, but the point is that many people never consider making banks compete to "earn" our loan. If you are qualified, and you are going through so much effort to make money for them, they should fight for your business. But we don't make them fight for it; we're happy they let us borrow. That is the bank making us qualify ourselves.

PUA's will demonstrate their value and spend significant time building and resisting a strong rapport with a woman. They will resist when she tries to make them qualify themselves, like she does with most men. Once she begins to show even the mildest attraction, the PUA then makes her jump through hoops to prove that she is worthy of his attention. "Pretty girls are a dime a dozen. Do you have any talents?"

A salesperson may seem unconvinced that the customer actually needs a service as high-caliber as the one he is offering and makes the customer provide reasons why that product would suit their needs better than a lower-grade alternative. The salesperson may also suggest that although most people buy Product A *(Affiliation)*, this customer seems like the type to buy a more modest product like Product B. The suggestion that buying Product B is a loss of Status makes them want to prove why Product A is better for them. Which was the salesperson's plan all along.

Hostage negotiators might turn the persuasion around by saying

"It would be a lot easier to secure your demands if you release a hostage to show that we can trust you." It sounds helpful, but the negotiator is actually making the criminal give something away.

In archetypical hero movies and legends (a "monomyth" or the "composite hero" identified by Joseph Cambell in the book *Hero With a Thousand Faces*) the main character is relunctant to be a hero, but he must make a difficult choice to follow his destiny.

Like Luke Skywalker in Star Wars or Neo in The Matrix, the main character of the story must be persuaded to greatness. This common plot device parallels the real-life feeling of getting a reluctant persuader to step forward and be the solution. Remember that a movie is persuading the audience, and we — as the audience — want Luke and Neo to be the solution, and their reluctance makes us want it even more! Luke Skywalker wanted to be a space pilot anyway; Neo was already searching for The Matrix. But we don't care. We're just happy when they say yes.

First and foremost, a persuader must resist the temptation to jump in and seize an opportunity once it has been exposed. As soon as a persuader reveals their cards, the persuasion is over and the other person gets permanent control. In Titanic, Jack didn't go in for the kill when Rose showed a little interest. He waited for her to come to him. The Army didn't say anything about going to war when they visited John's school. And Juan Mann didn't ask people to hold up a sign before they hugged him. It is important to make the person being persuaded feel like the decision was theirs. In fact, if persuasion is done perfectly, that's just the way it turns out.

To actually accomplish a turn around, most persuaders merely have to subtly take control of the conversation. "Controlling a conversation" is something that every telemarketer is taught in one way or another. Most often it just means that you become the person asking the questions and changing the subjects. However, there are also a few strategies for more interesting scenarios.

One excellent turn-around strategy is to ask a person how they would ideally like their need to be satisfied. For example, "when you bought your last barbecue, what were the things you liked most?" As obvious as it sounds on paper, in real life it comes across as a thoughtful question. You're helping them identify the type of thing that might solve their problem! You also happen to be eliciting a list of exactly what would persuade them the most. Once you know what they are looking for, you are able to become exactly that (reluctantly).

Once upon a time, when I used to book bands, I would tell club owners that the band was unavailable for any date that was close, even if the schedule was empty. It gave the impression that we were "booked solid" and they needed to accomodate us. We were eventually booked months in advance; a self-fulfilling prophecy.

Another good strategy is to help someone satisfy their need as if you're not an option. "Well, I have been in the industry for a long time, so I could help you find someone if you want. It's too bad I am so busy, or else I would be perfect for this project." The next thing out of their mouth is often something like "if you wanted to do it, when would you be available?" and then they are catering to you.

Occasionally it can be an effective strategy to actually say no, and then reverse your decision, if they can provide just one more thing...

The most counter-intuitive version of the turn-around or "bait and switch" happens when a person disagrees with you about their needs. If you have spent some time trying to create a need and the other person just doesn't agree that the need is "their" need, then you can agree with them, and begin to explain the ways in which you can see their point.

For example, if the neighbour's barbecue isn't quite enough to motivate the purchase of something new, start explaining why they should be happy with what they have. "Who needs to watch television and cook steaks at the same time? If we really want a television out here we can pull the little old one out of the basement. It's practically the same thing!" The end result is actually to draw attention to the weakness in their argument, by letting them hear it from someone else. It isn't as fun being right, when being right means being worse.

177

Remember that motivations are treated differently for ourselves than for "other people" which is why that approach works.

It is a high-value behavior and a strategic goldmine when you can create this scenario.

TRY THIS AT HOME

The key piece of the puzzle in Step 4 is Rapport. It is also easy to try in a lot of normal situations you will encounter. Next time you are around other people in any context (a party, meeting, date, bus stop, whatever) try to create rapport by mirroring the other person. Remember to start a conversation first!

If you get "caught" mirroring them it means you were "mimicking" them too closely. Just try again later, more subtly.

If you sit around a table with a group of people, try to choose your seat strategically so you can create rapport with someone specific. Watch their body language to see if it is "open" or "closed". Try to get them to open it by creating rapport, or by giving them a reason to open up (like a business card!).

Find something in common with anyone and use that to create rapport.

If you are creating rapport with someone as a way to create attraction, use "mixed signals" to be flirty. Mirror and agree a little, then push back with some indifference. Be the leader, not the follower.

If you get some good rapport going, try to shift your own body language to see if the other person will follow your lead. If so, success! If not, keep trying!

AVOID MANIPULATION

When it comes to being manipulated, this step is where the magic happens. If we like someone else, and they know our weaknesses, we're in trouble. The main problem is that when we are being persuaded and when we are being manipulated, Step 4 feels the same.

Motivations are a powerful thing, and they exist in the core of who we are. Motivations are intuition. If you have ever tried to "tell yourself" to do the right thing, when you badly want to do the fun thing, you know how hard it can be to say no to your primal impulses.

Freud's "defense mechanisms" included one called rationalization, which is easy to observe in real people. Many people misunderstand what this word means, and use it as if it means "to explain why I need it". As in: "I have to rationalize this purchase for the company." What it actually means is that people will create or accept any reason for why they "need" something that they already want. As a manipulator that is quite a tool to have in your toolbox.

If you really want a new car, even though your current car is in great condition, you may justify it to yourself by saying "I can definitely afford it" or "new cars get better mileage." The truth is, you want it. If you *needed* a new car you would have rode your bicycle or taken the subway to the dealership. If you're a car owner you might already be forming an argument in your head for this one.

My favourite use of the word "need" is for pure luxury items like diamond jewelery, which nobody needs, ever. "I need a present for all the hard work I've done." *(Status masquerading as Justice)* or "I need an engagement ring that shows how much you love me." *(Status masquerading as Love for a Mate)*

Fortune tellers are experts at creating a story that suits your core motivations, because nobody disagrees when they get what they want. If you miss a loved one so strongly that you visit a psychic, and the psychic tells you your loved one is happy and comfortable in the after-life and they miss you too, you feel great! For therapeutic reasons that is fine, but remember that you are paying someone to lie to you.

Entrepreneurs are often lured into "investing" in businesses with no hope of success, as long as the entrepreneur believes it is a unique opportunity that can only be recognized by someone with a keen business sense. They say to themselves "wait, I have a keen business sense!" and suddenly they can see the opportunity. Like a psychic, business people can often persuasively create the appearance of seeing opportunities before they happen.

Admit to yourself that your intuition can – and will – be wrong sometimes. You will save yourself manipulation and disappointment in the future.

SUMMARY

Creating rapport is one of the most vital elements of persuasion. It is a key part of all persuasive disciplines and includes three (almost) simultaneous parts: creating rapport, creating a need, and making the other person qualify themselves (the turn-around). These elements are otherwise known as making someone like you, need you, and want you.

Make them like you:

Creating rapport means mirroring and emulating the behavior of the other person, including posture, mood, and speech. This uses isopraxis to make them like you. Otherwise rapport is just being valuable and having a good attitude. Remember to resist rapport when adverse selection provides the other person with an advantage.

Make them need you:

Creating a need means highlighting a potential gain or potential loss via one of the 14 core motivations, but it is also possible to use a pre-existing need to our advantage.

Make them want you:

Making someone qualify themselves means turning the persuasion around so they begin to convince us that we should help them satisfy their motivations.

In Step 5: Isolation, we will learn that eliminating competing persuasive elements will drastically increase the chance of a successful persuasion.

STEP

05

Isolate

Remove competing messages or people.

FOCUS.

THIS IS IMPORTANT.

In many persuasions this is a "hidden" step because it is so necessary or so common that it is overlooked. Whether we call it "privacy" or "romance" or "confinement" this step is about isolating the person being persuaded.

In the previous step a persuader creates all the social tools needed for agreement, out of thin air. It is important that nothing distracts the person being persuaded from the ideas that have been built and the ideas that are about to be built in *Step 6: Convince*. Therefore, it is important to control what they think about and keep their attention on our message.

In extreme cases, isolation is vital to achieving the persuasion, manipulation, and brainwashing necessary to make people do big, drastic things. Interrogations happen in a private room. Business deals happen in a meeting room. Cult leaders and military training use private compounds to make sure everything has a singular theme. Psychopolitical movements brainwash their citizens by forcing some ideas onto them while prohibiting ideas that are free, creative, or contradictory (like in 1950's Communist Russia or North Korea right now).

Like many of these steps, we tend to have some natural, intuitive idea of how it works and the fact that we have to do it. When we have to tell someone something private we take them into another room or a quiet corner. We may whisper to a friend as they are about to make a risky decision and say "are you sure you want do this?" because whispering disallows other people.

Fortune tellers usually use a highly stylized private room or booth to give their readings, creating either a literal or figurative barrier between the reading and distractions. Televised psychics undoubtedly use the camera and/or editing to their advantage as well.

Movie theaters remove lighting and build walls that isolate outside sounds to make the viewing experience as immersing as possible. Most on-stage performances do something similar, and the fact that all seats face the same direction helps keep attention on the performers and not on interesting friends. Circular tables encourage talking and social contact, so if they exist in a theater they are typically placed closest to the stage for VIPs.

Sales, negotiations, and business meetings tend to happen in rooms created specifically for that purpose, or in the homes or offices of the people involved. Many people also conduct their business over the phone or via conference calls, which creates a certain level of isolation because no one else can participate properly.

On a well-designed website, the closer the customer gets to the final goal (often a purchase or a registration) the more focused and isolating the page becomes. Often the main menu is not available on payment pages, there are no banners, and additional content disappears from the periphery of the pages. This ensures that nothing else will tempt the customer to click away once they are moving toward their goal.

Cults recruit new believers by inviting them to private events, "getaways", dinners, and whatnot so they can convert those people without interruptions and distractions. And while surrounded by believers. It is a common element in all religions to bring new people into a group of believers before the new person becomes aware that the purpose is conversion, rather than simple friendship or entertainment. This is also why Mormons and Jehovah's Witnesses who go door-to-door have a much harder time converting anyone:

they try to isolate someone at home, on the doorstep, where they are most distracted and least interested in a religious message.

As a sidenote, they also don't establish rapport or needs, and they usually open with a blunt religious statement as well. Tsk, tsk.

Advertising, copywriting, political brainwashing, informercials, pick up artists, websites, speeches, popular music and many other forms of persuasion aren't able to – or just don't – effectively isolate their audience and therefore have much lower rates of success. These forms tend to rely on repetition instead – which is a poor man's persuasion – to increase the odds that you will experience the effect when you are already isolated. There is a reason they play "Top 40" songs 50 times a day.

Whether it is small kids in the background, or other people at your table, or just time to think for yourself, a lack of good isolation either has a diminished effect, or will "wear off" quickly as other thoughts and priorities enter the mind of the person being persuaded.

Isolation can be mild or extreme. Usually just taking someone aside is more than enough, but in general the level of isolation required to be effective is relative to the severity of the persuasion. Bigger persuasion, more isolation.

Regardless of how someone is isolated, the goal is to control information. Persuaders want to allow the other person to think about the persuasion as much as possible, because deeper thought creates more persuasive affect. What persuaders want to avoid is any competing persuasion. If you have ever been to an open market where merchants are yelling deals from every angle, you know what it's like to deal with more than one persuasion at a time.

Other people who disagree, other messages that disagree, or distractions that make it hard to concentrate should all be eliminated.

Three types of isolation can occur and each style can be very effective.

The three types of isolation are:

1. *Literal Isolation* – physically segregating someone from outside communication.
2. *Figurative Isolation* – creating a conversation "space" that feels like it is separate from everyone else.
3. *Social Isolation* – adding other people to surround the other person with many opinions that support our persuasion.

People gain a large part of their identity from the people around them. As we learned when we discussed motivations, Love, Status, Affiliation, and Justice play a huge part in our decision-making. By isolating someone, influences from other motivations (or motivating people) can be removed. Isolation also allows people to fulfill their real desires without any concern for what other people might think or feel about their choices.

Among the 8 Universal Steps of Persuasion this step is rather easy and understandable. Without it, a persuader may fail due to factors that are out of his control. With good isolation, the entire environment is the persuasion, and only the persuasion.

LITERAL ISOLATION

Generally speaking this is the most common and the most obvious type of isolation. If we literally or physically remove someone from other people and information they have no choice but to listen and absorb our information without much thought to competing ideas. From board rooms to prison cells, we isolate each other all the time.

In an interrogation room there is usually a complete lack of visual or emotional distractions; the interrogator is the focus. When prisoners misbehave they are put into solitary confinement. When someone is fired it happens in a private room to make it easier to maintain a calm, rational atmosphere.

With literal isolation, the key is merely to put a physical barrier between the persuasion and the world.

FIGURATIVE ISOLATION

While it may be slightly more difficult to achieve (only slightly), and slightly easier to break through, figurative isolation has the major advantage of being invisible. A person is free to come and go as they please, they can see other people and influences if they want – but they don't – because we have created an environment that supports our persuasion.

In a restaurant, background music at the perfect level can allow us to talk to other people at our table, while being unable to hear people at the table next to us. In fact, having separate tables for each party creates a "zone" where other people are not allowed, and it is usually considered rude to eavesdrop. Whispering uses a similar tactic to bring the volume of a conversation down below what other people can hear, and may also require us to stand close to the other person.

This is a sort of sensory isolation. It sends a signal to the room to "mind your business." If a persuader brings the other person around a corner, a similar effect is achieved.

Moving someone to a different part of the room is usually enough to create a feeling of privacy. PUAs will always separate their target from her friends eventually, taking her to a corner to talk more intimately. Sometimes when two people are flirting with each other the friends will leave them alone anyway, because we intuitively know it is hard to stay attracted when you have too many interruptions.

By telling people that bad things may happen outside of certain boundaries it can be possible to make people choose to figuratively isolate themselves. In M. Night Shyamalan's movie *The Village* an entire village of people are kept from exploring the wilderness around them because they believe the woods are full of monsters. This belief isolates them, without any actual physical boundaries.

In most religions there is some element of belief that non-believers are sinners, or not worthy, or ineligible for great rewards in the afterlife, which uses fear to isolate the believers within the religion. If you will suffer for not believing, you are much more likely to continue believing. Ironically, if you don't believe in the first place then you don't believe the punishment exists. One belief against another.

In countries that use psychopolitical tactics, communication from outside the country to blocked or restricted so the government can control what people now about "the outside". The less people know, the less they have to fight against. Its figurative isolation of an entire nation.

Figurative isolation can be as simple as acting like you would prefer to have a private conversation or it can be as elaborate as having your own compound, but regardless of the method, it is usually not something we are consciously aware of, and that is a major advantage for the persuader.

SOCIAL ISOLATION

The most difficult and most powerful form of isolation is to surround someone with other people who already agree with the goal of the persuasion. In cult recruitment this has been shown to turn someone from a non-believer into a fanatically loyal follower in about a week. Even when the new recruit is aware that they are being converted!

When we discussed value we learned that half of the value equation was for something to be desired by other people. If we provide a room, or city, or country full of people who we believe all want what we are being persuaded to want, the social pressure to agree can be overwhelming. Disagreeing with an entire group of people can create extreme anxiety, fear, and stress. When the quick and easy solution is just to agree, generally we agree.

Social isolation can be seen in cultures, fashion, languages, pop culture, and so on. Two small countries that share a border can have drastically different cultures, and those cultures keep them from intermingling. Fashion is radically different from social group to social group, and sometimes even defines social groups. If we want to be part of the group, we have to wear the right clothing *(Affiliation)*. Languages create a social barrier that makes it very difficult to communicate with each other. Sometimes people who speak a minority language use it to be rude or tell secrets in public, because no one else understands. Pop culture can isolate older generations from understanding younger generations, or social groups that share a niche interest sometimes have so much lingo within the interest, other people have no idea what they are talking about.

All of it is a form of social isolation, but it doesn't have be so broad to be effective. Two classes in the same school can be isolated from each other as they pass each other in the hall. Two groups of friends in the same class may barely know each other's names.

In 2009, at Chicago's Robeson High School, a total of 115 girls were pregnant. That was 1 out of 8 girls in a school that had about 800 girls. No single cause was known to have caused the pregnancies. This is an astonishing case because it is so rare for a high school to have such a high pregnancy rate. The social isolation of that school created an environment, apparently, where pregnancy and the behaviour that leads to pregnancy were acceptable and widespread. That sub-culture was unique, and while we could presumably blame economic and lifestyle factors, there are definitely other schools that share those factors and do not show such a high pregnancy rate.

Social isolation creates a temporary sub-culture, and within that sub-culture the rules can be anything; even things that are unacceptable in the "normal" culture that surrounds it.

The primary reason that kids begin smoking or drinking is that the social pressure is so strong. If we have 5 friends who all smoke, and bond over their smoking time together, and ridicule us for not smoking, it may just be a matter of time before we try it. Then the chemicals take over and addiction begins. Drinking alcohol is entirely a social event. People often make faces of disgust when they take a shot of something hard, but will do so repeatedly. It doesn't quench our thirst; it makes us thirstier. And if you have ever tried to go to a club with friends and resist drinking, your group will not only try to encourage you to have "just one," they may ask you what's wrong, or if you're feeling ok.

Fraternities use intense social pressure by having all pledges (applicants) perform the hazing (tests of humiliation) together, while enforced by a group of fraternity brothers. This social pressure can be so heavy that they perform illegal and immoral acts they would never consider otherwise. The ultimate reward of being accepted *(Affiliation and Status)* is enough to make them loyal to the frat for life.

If we go to a major sporting event and sit among the fans of the opposing team, we feel intimidated and might refrain from cheering for our team.

Social isolation is using the motivation of Status and Affiliation at the same time. "We will like you if you agree!"

We want to agree, even if we don't.

TRY THIS AT HOME

Isolating someone is easy and you probably do it regularly, if you think about it. Next time you want to talk to someone about anything, try to use a special room or area to do it. Or, if you can, get your friends to join in when convincing someone to "go with the herd".

Worst case scenario, just spend a day looking for people who are having conversations away from the main group, or people who agree because the group is watching.

AVOID MANIPULATION

Isolation isn't necessarily bad since it happens in persuasion, manipulation and brainwashing alike. However, when you are isolated it is much easier to be manipulated because there is no one else to be your voice of reason. Like with rapport, once you are motivated to agree, isolation can be the first nail in the coffin.

It can be easy for adults to think that only young people succumb to peer pressure, and it can be easy for young people to think that peer pressure only works on dumb people or weak people, but those opinions are incorrect. Adults are motivated to do damaging things all the time, and when you're young peer pressure is a way of life, not just in "isolated" events.

Never make a decision in isolation. Even during a completely positive persuasion, take a break and give yourself time to think through the decision you're about to make. Always get a second opinion from someone who cares about you or someone who is paid to care about you.

The more you like the idea of something, the more dangerous isolation can become. Just be careful.

It is also possible to isolate yourself, and this can lead to manipulation by yourself and others. I would argue that the reason this book exists is because experts in so many fields were too isolated to notice the pattern.

If you are isolated from other opinions and you are hesitating to commit to something, pause, reset, and leave the isolation. You will be able to think and decide more freely.

Because of Affiliation, we *want* other people to agree with us, so we may surround ourselves with people that agree, *because* they agree. This can make us feel good about bad decisions.

This often happens in the time leading up to an election, when people quietly believe that most people will vote for the candidate they think will win, even though nobody has said anything like that. The manipulative part is that they might vote for that candidate *because* they think everyone agrees, and not because it is the best candidate.

SUMMARY

In any persuasion we must remove competing influences for the best chance of success. This is achieved via one of the three types of isolation: literal, figurative, or social.

Literal Isolation:

In literal isolation we literally put barriers between a person and everything outside the persuasion.

Figurative Isolation:

In figurative isolation we use environmental factors to create an imaginary and invisible space in which the persuasion occurs.

Social Isolation:

In social isolation we use the motivations of Status and Belonging to create agreement by surrounding the other person with people that support our persuasion.

We have prepared ourselves with the proper knowledge, we have started a great conversation, and we have motivated the other person to see us as a trusted ally. Now it's time to explain our offer. In *Step 6: Convince*, we will learn how to present our case so it is engaging and easy to understand. We will also look at a list of quick-and-dirty tricks from the experts to make information more persuasive in daily life.

STEP
06

Convince

Present a simple, engaging argument.

FACTS ARE IMPORTANT.

FEELINGS ABOUT FACTS ARE MORE IMPORTANT.

After doing the research for this book, I no longer believe in "rational arguments".

Educated people and critical thinkers may require rational information to be convinced they agree, but it is not what makes them agree.

Most often people will ask for rational evidence, and know consciously that they will be convinced by it if the persuader can provide it. Which raises an interesting question: If you know at some point while being persuaded that the right numbers or facts will convince you, haven't you already been persuaded?

Scientists, analysts, and other people that make their living based on hard facts and data will resist this, but when presented with data that strongly goes against their beliefs, they — like all people — will immediately search for other explanations or even feel disappointed. That's when denial may appear.

If a doctor says you are "morbidly obese" you might cry. The doctor has merely stated a medical fact and placed you into a true medical category. We shouldn't feel anything about a strict fact, but in this case most people would feel shame or sadness.

The point is: we can *feel* something about *facts*.

When people think of "persuading" they usually think of this step. The typical person will want to get to the convincing step as soon as possible, because they believe that Step 6 is where the magic happens.

It's not.

It's where the hard work happens.

We have already discussed how important it is for the persuader to have rapport, and the purpose of rapport is so that the other person trusts the persuader and believes the persuader and wants the persuader to be right. People hear what they want to hear, and when Step 4 is done properly the other person wants to hear things that convince them. They are already biased. Psychologists would say they are *primed.*

If that bias wasn't important you could convince someone who hates you and thinks you're a liar just by providing a few facts and figures. Good luck with that. What will happen in real life is that they will refuse to believe the objective information and stick to their beliefs or intuition instead. Science vs. religion is intensely controversial for a reason.

If the other person has been hesistating thus far, and rapport and motivations have been done well, this is the step where their mind will be changed. With good rapport and needs, hesitation is usually because other forces are competing with the persuader (due to weak Isolation). The business executive who says "give me something to tell my boss" is already open to being convinced; he just needs more than a feeling to work with. That's what Step 6 is for.

If our persuasion hasn't gained enough to momentum on its own to succeed before we make it to *Step 6: Convince*, then we are either doing a long-term persuasion, a high-threshold persuasion (explained in this chapter), or we got carried away with ourselves and moved through the previous steps too quickly.

If a persuader ever feels like they're pushing themselves on someone, or if it feels unexpected to explain the details, it's probably that they've rushed the previous steps. Rapport is a vital and important factor in persuasion, and you can never have too much of it. If the person we are persuading isn't motivated to be convinced, we're wasting our time anyway.

Step 6 includes presentational techniques from teaching, hypnosis, songwriting, screenplay writing, sales, and negotiation, among others. Disciplines which all benefit from making people understand and absorb information in a memorable way.

If we're doing a long-term persuasion, like getting a promotion or making someone fall in love, then this step is when we'll build a fortress around the fragile perception of need and rapport we have already established. The first key is to present the information in gradual stages, so that each successive step is easy to understand, digest, and agree with.

The persuader will also need to ensure that the information never gets boring or repetitive as they work their way through the convincing. For that, every persuader needs to understand the balance between being predictable enough to be coherent, but unpredictable enough to be interesting.

In a high-threshold persuasion the persuader has their work cut out for them, and it will be necessary to understand how threshold works in general.

Convincing people sometimes requires "the right thing at the right time" and at the end of this step I have provided a list of quick-and-dirty ingenious tips & tricks – collected from a wide range of persuasive disciplines – for making an argument more persuasive.

Oh, and before we get into the mechanics of how threshold works, here's a tip: if you're going to try to convince someone, you have to know what you're talking about. If you are persuading for sales, or as a fortune teller, or any other type of expert, or consultant, or authoritative work, know your stuff and know it well. Shaky credibility can become rock solid if a person opens their mouth and reliability comes out.

THRESHOLD

Threshold is a crucial and simple idea for understanding how

IF YOU WERE RIGHT, I'D AGREE WITH YOU.

ROBIN WILLIAMS
ACTOR/COMEDIAN

difficult it will be for someone to agree to our persuasion. The short version is: the more the other person needs to do to agree, the higher the threshold. In some industries this is also referred to as "friction" or "resistance".

A trend you have undoubtedly picked up on by now is that persuasion is about 10% of what we want, and 90% what the other person wants. Threshold is 100% from the point of view of the other person, and the persuader must reduce the perception of threshold as much as possible.

If a salesperson is selling a car for $20,000, they have to be much more persuasive than if they are selling a postcard for 99¢. The postcard may not require a "convincing" step at all, whereas the car may require test drives, meetings, time to think about it and compare, negotiation, facts and figures, testimonials from other drivers, and some general ass-kissing to make the sale.

In general it is easier to get agreement for a small decision with a low threshold than for a big decision with a high threshold. If there are examples to the contrary, I have not seen them.

If we want someone to let us wash their car for $5, then threshold is $5 and a little bit of trust; not a lot of convincing. If we need a loan from the bank then a fair bit more convincing is required. If we want someone to marry us, usually a whole relationship worth of convincing (or an equivalent amount of booze) has been necessary. And if we want someone to surrender their identity and become a loyal follower of a cult they have never heard of, well, it's going to take a lot of extremely persuasive convincing.

Most often we can't change how big the threshold is overall. If you're buying a car, you're going to have to pay for it one way or another. What a persuader can do is change two things about the perception of the threshold:

1. The big agreement can be broken into several smaller agreements instead

2. The effort it takes to actually agree (or "close") can be reduced.

For example if you're buying a car, the purchase might begin with a test drive. You're not buying it yet, you're just trying it. This will increase your need for the car (hopefully) and also allow the salesperson to point out the many benefits while you experience them. Plus there is the new car smell. When you leave the test drive and get back into your old crappy car it feels like a little loss, doesn't it?

Also, perhaps the cost of the car can be broken into small monthly payments. Instead of $20,000 it's only $199/month, and you can easily afford that! Plus with the better mileage, it practically pays for itself! Now that big commitment seems much more manageable as several smaller commitments instead. But let's make it even easier...

To reduce the friction between you and agreement, we could provide you with our simple in-house credit! No need to give any money now, just take it home for free. In fact you don't have to pay us anything for 6 months! It's like there is no cost at all. Spend that time saving up some money (yeah right) and you'll always be ahead of your payments. You won't even notice it. In fact, if you trade in your old car we can make the monthly fees even lower and you can drive your new car home right now! I'll even throw in air conditioning for free.

Ok, snap out of it! Everything you just read since the two ways to change the perception of threshold has been convincing elements (in a slightly sarcastic tone).

Even though it might feel easier to get the car now, *nothing has changed*. The price has actually increased because now you're paying with credit, which has interest. Your old car was undoubtedly traded for less than you could get in a private sale (the price the dealership will sell it for). And although you don't pay for 6 months, that doesn't effect the actual amount of debt. Interest might even be accruing the whole time.

But it *feels* easier. And that's the point. If the dealership said "$20,000 take it or leave it." We would be significantly less likely to consider buying it.

Through the eyes of the other person, start to think about the main obstacles for agreement to take place. Is there a cost involved?

Perhaps some effort required? Maybe a long, tedious form to fill out? Do they have to rat out their friend to go free? When we sign the contract, are we then committed to 2 years of service?

Specifically, we will want to look at the 14 motivations from the other person's point of view. In some cases the only downside is that the other person must switch from something they understand to something they don't, but it can be enough to make them perceive the threshold to be too high to agree. In which case, explaining it simply or giving a free demonstration makes all the difference in the world.

As we proceed with convincing someone, the goal is to make them understand why the potential gain is so great, and to eliminate the threshold/cost/effort/risk. When trying to convince people to switch from a PC to a Mac, for example, the key is to show them how simple it can be to switch, or if possible, to teach them how to use a Mac before they switch, making the threshold nearly zero. If you could throw in a free transfer of their files, even better! Easier said than done? Sure. But not difficult.

In that example, a lifelong PC user has no idea what the difference is with a Mac. They can't imagine it or understand it because they have no information and no experience with a Mac, and are likely to assume that it is the same as their PC, just different, like Coke and Pepsi. Why switch? The job of Apple is to fix that gap of information, and to do it using the 14 motivations. Don't sell features, sell benefits.

BABY STEPS
(or "progressive presentation")

In a low-threshold persuasion it may only be necessary to give a reason why you would like the other person to agree. For example if your goal is to get a drive to the store to get milk, then having rapport and saying please before you ask (politeness is a teeny tiny gift of Status to the other person) might be enough.

On the other hand, a high-threshold persuasion may require

months of convincing or at least a Powerpoint presentation. In this situation it can be difficult to merely ask for the entire goal all at once.

A politician could never just take the podium the day before an election and say "vote for me!" and expect to win against a candidate that had spent months showing why his values and ideas are worth voting for (creating rapport). PUA's spend hours working from playful hand touches, to flirtatious touching or tickling, to kissing and sex. A cult leader begins with a simple invitation for fun, then an innocent lecture, then a week-long trip to a ski lodge, then a percentage of your family income. And at McDonald's they make millions of dollars per year by asking if you would like to "super size" a meal you've already intended to buy, for only 59 cents more.

Drastically re-designing a website can cause an upheaval among its users, but adding or changing new features one at time over a year or two generally causes very little feedback at all, because nobody realizes how far they've come, one little step at a time. Over time Facebook has learned that lesson the hard way.

Progressive presentation or "baby steps" are directly related to reducing the perception of threshold, as we examined above. However, it also creates a sturdy pyramid of learning where the other person understands the basics first, them more details, then more details, and finally the most impressive technicalities. It's how experts become experts!

Structuring your presentation so it is progressive, using baby steps, or phases, or a logical sequence makes the entire presentation much easier to absorb. Making each step as simple as possible makes the person being persuaded feel like every small agreement was obvious. I may not understand how to build an airplane now, but by teaching me the principles, and working with models, and building one component at a time, then combining them, and the working with real planes... over a period of several years I will have learned to build a plane one step at a time, and I will have understood each step along the way. This is how every school on the planet operates (some better than others), because it is how humans learn.

The simplest structure we can use for a presentation is the 3-Step model described best by Will Smith's character in the movie *7 Pounds*:

1. Tell them what you're going to tell them.
2. Tell them.
3. Tell them what you told them.

And it really can be as simple as that. The key idea is not to tell people the same thing three times, but to prepare people for everything one step at a time, in a progression.

During an introduction ("tell them what you're going to tell them") we can only give the general idea in simplistic terms and without any details. However, we can tell them what to expect, and we can be strategic about it. If we want them to view our presentation as a vision of the future, then we should tell them that we are presenting a vision of the future. If we intend it to be a short-term plan or a long-term plan, we should tell them. And if they have asked us to present something in particular ("show me a design for a sofa that is feminine and traditional") then we should tell them we are about to show them what they asked for. Whether or not they think we have succeeded in presenting that is a question of quality, and that's up to you.

In a word, we're giving the other person context.

What the persuader should not do in the introduction is tell the other person how much they are going to like something, or how amazing it is. There are two reasons for this. First, if they disagree, the persuader looks extra stupid. Second, it takes away the ability for them to be impressed; at best they can agree that is was great, which is much less fun. This is especially true if the presentation is something of the persuader's own creation, because then they sound egotistical by evaluating their own work as "excellent". The persuader can express their pride or enthusiasm, but let the other person form opinions of their own.

When the introduction has been laid out cleary and simply, and the persuader begins to explain the meat of the offer, the rules change. Emotional content, things that are memorable or amazing, and unique information is exactly what we should provide, especially if we can create a new way of seeing an old idea. Complimentary language like "great", "amazing", "unbelieveable" and so on have a large effect on the perception of the audience. Steve Jobs, the former CEO of Apple, was a master of this technique.

One interesting thing about giving an argument is that the more educated a person is, the more they may be looking for solid reasoning. However all people respond equally well to the 14 motivations. Therefore we should always maintain the emotional and motivational value in our presentations, and if we have educated listeners, we can also provide some facts and figures to chew on. That being said, make "data" as visual as possible and keep it short and sweet; even accountants get bored looking at balance sheets for an hour.

Keep the 14 motivations in mind at all times, and as you build your offer from the ground to the sky, make sure each step is easy to agree with and attached to the motivation of the other person. If you have established a particular motivation as the need, this is your chance to twist the knife by providing specific examples of how that motivation will benefit if they agree.

The end result should be that they get progressively more and more motivated until they can't wait to agree.

PERSUASIVE RHYTHM

Boredom will kill any persuasion. In my mind Microsoft Powerpoint is synonymous with boredom, because people tend to use it as notes for themselves instead of a presentation for everyone else. So the experience for the audience is slide after slide after slide of text....zzzzzzz.

A movie with no drama or action or romantic tension or suspense tends to make us lose our focus. Somewhere in the middle of the movie we seem to detach from the plot and start rationally thinking about the movie itself. The experience is dead.

A comedian must build his jokes in a way that the audience "gets it". They must understand the context, then think they see something coming, and then BAM! Unexpected punchline. Hilarious!

Boredom exists when something is too predictable. It has a pattern that repeats the way you expect. Once the audience understands the pattern they know what comes next, and people are pretty good at noticing patterns. The Catch-22 is that if something isn't repetitive enough it is confusing and hard to organize, mentally. So where do persuaders draw the line?

The key is to *almost* create patterns and for that we have to understand when a pattern happens.

People will generally notice when something has happened twice in a row. If that "something" is a little more complicated or happens quickly, it might take three times in a row. Whether it has happened twice or three times, our brains pick up on the repetition and expect it to repeat again. In fact, this is a common element on IQ tests; how well can you spot a pattern in progress.

Brains are fascinating when it comes to patterns. If a stimulus or pattern is new or "novel" our attention is drawn to it. It's interesting. We want to see if it is what we think it is, or how it is different from what we think it is. The fascinating part is that if it does turn out the way we expected and continues to do so, our brain tunes it out. It gets boring and we tend to ignore it. For example, if you create "white noise" in a room (a quiet, soothing static noise, like 'snow' on TV) you will notice it immediately at the beginning. 10 minutes later it will have disappeared and the entire room seems quieter. Your brain made it disappear because it was so repetitive and reliable; you didn't need it anymore.

Now you know what happens to Powerpoint presentations.

The trick is to change the pattern exactly when the audience thinks they have it figured out. If you continue to do this, they continue to be interested.

Have you ever wondered why one song sucks and another song is catchy? Maybe not, but the structure of songs, television, movies, stage performances, sporting events and other forms of entertainment provide us with a valuable lesson about structuring experiences to be engaging.

Let's look at the structure of a children's song as an example:

Three blind mice
Three blind mice

See How They Run
See How They Run

They all ran after the farmer's wife
She cut off their tails with a carving knife
Have you ever seen such a thing in your life, as

Three blind mice

There are some obvious groupings in these lyrics, and the melody follows them exactly. We can divide this rhyme into a few parts to make it easier to discuss.

A = "Three blind mice"
B = "See how they run"
C = "They all ran after the farmer's wife
       She cut off their tails with a carving knife
       Have you ever seen such a thing in your life, as"

Then what we get for the structure of this rhyme is: AA BB C A.

'A' happens twice, so we expect it to happen again. But it doesn't.

Instead we get B, which happens twice as well, and with a similar melody (but a little higher). Now if we stopped the song there, a first-time listener might expect another part with a similar melody to start and happen twice. But it doesn't.

The C part jumps to a higher note than expected, has an unexpected melody and rhythm, and happens 3 times instead of 2. It's completely different! Then how does the song end?

With A again. And it is somehow very satisfying.

The reason this song and its rhymes and melody feel catchy and satisfying is that it *almost* creates patterns. Modern pop music and even Mozart pieces use this same patterning (in a much more advanced way) to create elaborate pieces of music that are interesting for minutes at a time.

To see how easily this song can become boring, try doubling each part. Like this:

Three blind mice
Three blind mice
Three blind mice
Three blind mice

See How They Run
See How They Run
See How They Run
See How They Run

They all ran after the farmer's wife
They all ran after the farmer's wife
She cut off their tails with a carving knife
She cut off their tails with a carving knife
Have you ever seen such a thing in your life
Have you ever seen such a thing in your life, as

Three blind mice
Three blind mice

In a short song like this, doubling each part is not a drastic change, but immediately it starts to get more "irritating" than "catchy". If we doubled it again, everyone you sang it to would be aggravated by the end, if they made it that far.

A persuader must realize that repetition is good for making something memorable, and for letting people absorb the information in stages (progressive presentation), but too much repetition is no longer useful.

In movies there are plot points called "pinches" where the characters are faced with an unexpected problem that must be solved or handled. Although it is relevant to the story, it was unexpected, and the audience becomes highly engaged until the pinch has been resolved.

The long intermission in a hockey game or baseball game doesn't happen in the middle, it happens closer to the end. By that point in the game the audience knows who is winning and what has to be done for the underdog to survive. Halftime at the Super Bowl includes a big show and advertising that has been specially crafted, just to keep the audience interested.

Broadway shows happen in three acts, with an intermission after the second (like a hockey game). By that time the climax has happened and the intermission only creates positive tension before the satisfying ending. The intermission is the theater equivalent of the "C part" in Three Blind Mice. It breaks the pattern and delays the satisfying conclusion of the pattern.

The same can be done when convincing.

A pick-up artist typically has "routines" that involve card tricks, or psychological games, or palm reading, or anything else that might be fun for a few minutes. However, most of a "pick up" is just conversation. The PUA and the girl might talk about anything at all, and although the PUA has strategic elements in every topic, the girl needs to feel like it is getting better and better. Therefore the games and routines are interspersed throughout the interaction to keep everything lively and exciting. Combined with the progressive nature of flirting, it's very immersing. She never has a chance to get bored.

Comedians will sometimes cleverly tell a joke so that we think its over and then several minutes later make another reference to it, and it's even more hilarious. If they had told it all together: not as hilarious.

If a persuader were explaining the features of a new hot tub, she might start by explaining each place a person can sit or lay in the hot tub. Perhaps a seat for every type of person. Then she could go around again to each seat, this time explaining the functions available to the person in that position. If the third set of examples also mentioned each position and a feature again, it starts to get repetitive and boring.

That would be a good time to talk about the built-in mini-fridge instead, that only the host can reach, making that person the life of the party *(Status)*.

To finish the presentation in a satisfying way she could revisit each person in the hot tub yet again, explaining how different seating for different people encourages good conversation and social experiences, and each seat has a special place for drinks served by the host. Every time the seating was used as a "motif" for presentation the information got more and more elaborate (progressive presentation).

In the end the person will remember exactly what types of seats are in the hot tub and exactly what can be done in each.

Anytime we take two pieces of similar information and repeat them or we make two logical, expected steps, we are getting close to a pattern and should consider throwing in a curveball, or shifting to a new two-step section.

Remember: When information is presented really quickly it may take people three examples to notice and anticipate the pattern (which you will also notice in faster music).

PUTTING IT ALL TOGETHER

If you actually sung the rhyme out loud to yourself you may have also noticed that the melody starts low for the A section, gets a little higher for the B part, and then jumps even higher for the C part. This is a progressive or "baby steps" structure as well.

The ideal presentation breaks a large agreement into smaller segments. Each segment is something that seems obvious and easy, making it easy to agree to the whole persuasion in steps, rather than all at once. From segment to segment of convincing, the "presentation" should get progressively more detailed and more informative. Every time the presentation seems to have a predictable "next step" that is the perfect time to include an unexpected element, especially if it can be something fun or exciting by itself. Worst case scenario, take a break when a pattern seems unavoidable.

When used properly together, the progressive "baby steps" method and the persuasive rhythm method combine to be very engaging and easy to absorb.

TRY THIS AT HOME: TIPS & TRICKS

While researching so many varieties of persuasion I came across a lot of great little tips and tricks that might be the "right thing at the right time", even if they won't make or break a persuasion by themselves. They may not all fit every persuasive context, but if they are helpful to you, use 'em!

Here is a selected list of curiously clever and downright devious techniques:

Give it a name.
By giving something a name or making it a euphemism, a persuader controls the way it is perceived. For example, at the end of a date, when a girl asks a guy in for "coffee" they both know that nobody

is going to have coffee until the next morning. By giving the actual goal a seemingly innocent name, the threshold has been lowered, and it can be discussed more freely, even when both parties know exactly what is going on.

It also allows the girl to say, "I invited him in for coffee, and one thing led to another..." rather than admitting she had that plan all along. Euphemisms allow us to detach from taboos and forbidden subjects as well as making bad things seem more tolerable. Governments love this technique.

Misdirect attention.

Magicians are the masters of literal misdirection. They make you look in one place even though the action happens somewhere else. In the end things seem to occur by "magic".

Controlling someone's attention can be a powerful tool in persuasion. People tend to focus on goals rather than journeys, so if you give people a goal, like an award or certification, they may overlook the fact that they have to use your product to get certified or pay to be considered for an award.

Use probability against intuition.

It is fairly common to use someone's intuition against them by creating a situation where the intuitive "odds" and the actual "odds" are different. A great example is the Monty Hall Problem where a contestant must "pick a door" on a game show.

Imagine you have three doors and one contains a prize. You pick a door, but before they open it, the host does you a favour and eliminates one of the remaining doors (because he obviously knows which door contains the prize).

Then you are given a choice: would you like to keep the door you chose, or would you like to take the other remaining door? There are two doors left, so it seems you have a 50/50 chance of being right...

...but wait, let's back up a step. Before you chose anything, the odds that it was in any of the doors was 1 in 3 (33.3% chance) for

I USE EMOTION FOR THE MANY AND RESERVE REASON FOR THE FEW.

ADOLF HITLER
NAZI LEADER

every door. How come the odds are 50/50 now? Actually, they're not. And in this situation you should always choose to switch doors.

When you picked a door, the odds were 33.3% that it was that door, and 66.7% that it wasn't. When the host eliminated a door, the odds are still 66.7% that it is not in your door.

33.3% your door, **66.7%** not your door.

Only one door is not your door now, so you should switch. 33.3% of the time you'll be wrong, but 66.7% of time you'll be right.

Pigeons get this right, but most people don't switch, because their door is "their" door *(Affiliation: Territorial)* and they think they are right *(Status)*.

Oops. Intuition fails again.

My other favourite example of this technique is when fortune tellers "see" addresses and the client supplies the meaning. If I "see an address with a 6, or maybe a 9" it can include most houses on a street. The numbers 6 or 9, or 16 or 19, 26 or 29, and so on, are all possible matches. The address could be the client's house, the client's neighbour, or even an address that could be seen from their house or neighbour's house. With two similar numbers like 6 and 9, it covers almost every house on almost any street in almost any neighbourhood.

But it's amazing when they "know" things that are as personal as your childhood best friend's address!

Oversell with multiples.

It is extremely common in grocery stores to sell things in multiples. Instead of offering 1 item for $5, the sign says "2 for $10". Mathematically the cost is the same either way, but psychologically it has changed.

First of all, the store has created a slight social pressure by implying that you're "not allowed" to buy 1 item, when of course you are. Second, you are now thinking of buying more than one, which you might not have considered originally. Interestingly, most people will buy 2 or 4 or 6. Even if they only need 1 or 3.

This is done by the store because they are able to calculate how many of these items the "average" person buys. If that is less than 2 per visit, they make a deal on 2 items. The store makes more money per visit and raises the average value per purchase.

I have even seen a store sell items "2 for $10" when the cost for a single item is $4.75, which is just evil.

Compare to something worse.

Everyone has seen a discounted price tag where the store shows the original price crossed out in favour of a new "sale" price. "Was $500, now $200". The problem is that there is no way to confirm that the "original price" was ever actually charged. The "original price" could just be an invented number, and sometimes it is.

Remember that motivations are relative. A deal seems better because it is lower than what we are used to, or lower than what we think it is actually worth. If the store shows a price that is much higher, but we can have it for a major discount, more people will buy. The deal seems better.

Informercials do this as well when they offer you "A $99 value for only $19.95!" Who determined it is a $99 value?

I have even seen stores have a sale on "selected items" and raise the price on everything else, because they know that when there is a sale, our brains stop working.

Create positive tension.

There is a time and place for making people wait. If the threshold of something is very low, or if you know that someone is anticipating a gain of some kind, making them wait for it can achieve two things.

First, it makes the final result even more satisfying. Second, while they are waiting they are much more likely to buy or agree to things related to what they are waiting for, just so they can feel closer to having it.

Stores, movies, and concerts even use lines of people waiting for tickets as a PR asset. News programs and newspapers are eager to write about a crowd of people waiting for a movie to premier or the next Harry Potter book to go on sale.

When we break a pattern to keep things interesting during Step 6, we have to break it with something different, and positive tension is often the result. We want the expected conclusion, but we don't get it. Yet.

Romantic comedies are notorious for making one of the main character screw up just as it seems everything is going to work out, and they have to race to undo their mistake in time for... the end of the movie.

Set the standard.

The relativity of motivations strikes again! People will typically make choices based on what they feel is "normal" *(Affiliation)*. They want to be at least as normal as everyone else, and maybe just a liiiittle better. Or a lot better. *(Status)*

By setting a "standard" a persuader can give people a reference point that is pulled completely from thin air, on which to base their decision. For example, if you are asking for donations and "suggest" a donation of $5, you'll probably get a lot of $5 donations. If you "suggest" a $20 donation, you may not get a lot of $20 bills, but you'll definitely get more $10 bills.

Use metaphors.

Storytelling can be a great way to make people "see the light". The main reason is that metaphors don't actually contain a lot of information about our actual situation, but people can "connect the dots" between the two.

A metaphor makes the other person feel like something makes sense, when in reality the listener is making it make sense. For example I might say: "Diplomacy is a weapon against war itself, and that is why we need more resources for diplomats."

In your head, you connect parallels between needing weapons to fight a war, and needing diplomacy to fight war. If you don't have

217

enough weapons you certainly can't fight a war, so we must need more diplomacy to fight against war itself!

It sounds good, but in reality, do you know that more diplomacy is a way to stop war? Do you know that we don't have "enough" now? What are these "resources" we're discussing? What do we mean by "diplomacy" anyway, isn't that a process? How is a process a weapon? Isn't war a process too? How do you fight against a process?

Metaphors create false analogies that seem obvious and true, but aren't. The innocent use of a metaphor can be great to connect two ideas. Icarus got cocky, flew too close to the sun, and failed. Don't make the same mistake!

Many metaphors are not as innocent as they sound, but they work well anyway.

Say it with quotes.

When you make a statement about something in your own words, that opinion is only as good as your reputation. But if you say it in the words of someone else, now your opinion is as good as theirs.

I could tell you that it is important to try new ways of persuading people if you don't get the results you're looking for, and most people would probably agree that that is a reasonable statement.

But someone like Einstein might be more influential...

Use Statistics.

Stats are a double-edged sword. As someone who deals with a lot of statistics on a daily basis I will be the first to tell you that they can be just as confusing as they are effective. But that's not why you should use them.

Statistics hide a lot of effort behind a single number. And most stats can be organized into attractive, visual presentations (charts, infographics, etc.). In the book *Freakonomics* by Steven Levitt and Stephen J. Dubner, they present several fascinating cases of how economics and statistical analysis can be used in unconventional ways. I have (relatively) no doubt that their statistics are reliable, but to check that assumption would take more information, resources and know-how than I have available to me. Like most statistics, most of the time.

In real life we just don't check. Whether statistics are completely true or false, we just read them and continue drawing conclusions.

In reality many statistics are calculated badly, or in a way that is biased, to give us a certain impression. "This concert will bring in over $1 Billion to the local economy." That seems like a massive, broad number to just whip up when needed. It doesn't matter to the stats-maker whether it is accurate or not, because the objective is to create a number that is persuasive. Are you going to be the town councillor that says "I don't care about a billion dollars, it will destroy the biggest park in the city"?

Climb the Yes Ladder.

One very clever combination of psychology and progressive presentation is a Yes Ladder. When a person says "yes" to several things in a row, they are more likely to continue saying "yes" to further things. It is part positive attitude and part habit-formation, one could say.

Now imagine that at several times during the convince step you get the other person to agree to, or confirm mundane details. "Are you comfortable? ...Can I refill your water? ...Shall we get started? ...This is our first slide, can you see it well from there? ...Would you agree that your top competitors have a strong position?"...Etc.

So far those are all agreements to questions with no real content. Warm-up yes's. Later in the presentation when a persuader asks something like "do you think this sounds like something your brand could use?" the empty questions have seemlessly shifted into more meaningful questions that imply small commitments.

Eventually, when it comes time to close (Step 7), the probability of getting a "yes" is higher.

INSANITY IS DOING THE SAME THING OVER AND OVER, EXPECTING DIFFERENT RESULTS.

ALBERT EINSTEIN
THEORETICAL PHYSICIST

Use positive phrasing.

Phrasing sentences in a positive way can change the tonality of a whole document or speech, while it also makes information clearer.

Positive phrasing would be saying "I like the blue one." Negative phrasing would be "I don't like the red one."

First and foremost, positive phrasing keeps everyone in a constructive frame of mind by focusing on things that matter, rather than the things that don't. However, if I asked you which one you like, and your answer was "I don't like the red one," I still don't know which one you like, even though you gave me an answer.

It can be tempting, especially when giving feedback or criticism about something, to focus on the things that are wrong. After a whole presentation about mistakes though, we are left without a way to move forward. This can increase the threshold by making your presentation seem critical and unproductive.

Be silent.

There is no specific technique to describe here other than, sometimes the best thing to say is: nothing.

For example, sometimes while a colleague or teammate is persuading someone we think of something that they haven't mentioned. What if that is something the client wants to know?! Suddenly all we can focus on is an opportunity to jump in and speak our mind.

Relax. Silence is often a sign of contemplation and confidence. Rather than assuming the persuasion is crumbling beneath you, stay silent. When there is a pause, ask if there are any questions to see if anyone brings it up. It might be all in your head.

There is no such thing as a "strong, noisy type". So keep your composure, stay quiet and observe, instead of solving problems that might not exist.

Offer two ways to agree.

A Double Agreement is a question or choice that has multiple options, all of which are good for you. If you know your way around fallacies you will notice that these create a false dichotomy, or a choice between two things that aren't mutually exclusive. In other words, you could choose both or neither, but those dont seem like options at the time.

The basic idea is to have someone agree to something before knowing where you're going with your thought. Such as: "You seem adventurous, would you agree?" You would ask this presuming that they will say yes. Once they do, the persuader walks them into a trap. "You said you were adventurous, so you will want to try this."

Now there is an implication that adventurous people like what you're about to explain. If the other person doesn't like it, they are not adventurous. If they are adventurous (as they claim) then they will like it. Their options are: agree, or admit they lied about being adventurous.

Some other famous examples include:

"If this doesn't work for you, you're doing it wrong."

The options are: it works or you don't.

"Believers go to heaven, everyone else goes to hell."

The options are: believe in heaven or believe in hell. Either way, believe.

"I only date girls who can cook, can you cook?"

The options are: You can't cook, or I'm going to date you.

If you ever get stuck in a double agreement, ask yourself one question: Are my two options opposites? If they're not, it's a false dichotomy. If they are, ask if those are the only options. For example, not believing in heaven or hell would solve your problem immediately.

Re-frame with Verbal Judo / Aikido.

Sometimes someone gives you an objection during Step 6 that

seems impossible to overcome. Many books deal with this concept, but my favorite example is from a book called *Modern Persuasion Strategies* by Donald J. Moine and John H. Herd.

Imagine you have been presenting a pitch to a CEO and his board of managers. Their company has been steadily declining for a couple years now, and you are trying to convince them to use you as a supplier instead. The managers all agree that this is a good decision, but the CEO is not convinced.

After the meeting, you speak with him privately and ask what exactly he doesn't like about your pitch (like any high-value person would). He says that he has been using this supplier since the beginning and loyalty is one of his strongest values. At first glance it may seem as if you are stuck.

The technique of re-framing is about using someone's objection as the reason why they should agree. To do this you need to take the momentum of that idea and use it to your advantage, which is why it is also called Verbal Judo /Aikido.

In this case, the persuader told the CEO that loyalty was also one of his strongest values, and that all suppliers should be lucky enough to have a loyal client such as him. The question the CEO had to ask himself was: who is he more loyal to, the old supplier or his company and managers who want a new supplier?

In the end the CEO agreed and switched suppliers.

It isn't always necessary to disagree with someone to change their mind. Sometimes agreeing with an objection is the strongest position a persuader can have.

Maximize or minimize stress.

This technique comes from the world of criminal interrogation when a criminal is trying to keep himself out of trouble and the interrogator wants a confession. It is purely a method of manipulating emotions to encourage irrational decisions.

When a criminal (or a liar, for that matter) has done something wrong but they won't admit it, they are already in a stressful spot.

When they know that someone else suspects them, it becomes very stressful.

Maximizing is merely a matter of "helping" them be stressed by emphasizing how bad it is and how intolerable it must be to keep it all inside. Ultimately the goal is to make them want to confess, just to feel the relief of not carrying the guilt anymore.

Minimizing is similar but opposite. If someone has done something quite bad and they know that the punishment will be severe, it might help for the interrogator to make them feel as if it isn't nearly as bad as it seems. Sure they committed the crime, but most people would have done the same given the circumstances. Basically, when someone is desperate, if you validate and support their belief that it could still turn out ok, a confession might be easier for them to provide.

As a real life example, if you believe that your spouse has cheated, one of these strategies might work to extract a confession. Maybe you should maximize how horrible it would be for a cheater to carry that knowledge knowing that every day is one big lie to their spouse. Or to minimize, maybe you can imply that you can understand how people might need to cheat once or twice to keep a relationship happy in the long run, and that as long as the spouse knows, you're sure it wouldn't be a big deal.

Whether it is a trap for a cheater or an interrogation, once the confession is made, it doesn't matter what made them confess, the consequences are the same.

Prepare like a negotiator.

Professional negotiators have a frame of mind (and a bit of research) that prepares them for Step 6 better than most persuaders, and it revolves around the idea of knowing the other person's situation well. It is necessary for them to be a little more aware of the "big picture" than a typical persuader, because they make a living persuading other persuaders.

Professional persuaders often represent large organizations when they enter a negotiation, and since everybody knows exactly what is happening, it tends to be both competitive and cooperative in nature. Ideally, everybody will be happy when they leave the room.

Negotiators work with two acronyms: BATNA and WATNA which stand for Best Alternative to a Negotiated Agreement and Worst Alternative to a Negotiated Agreement. In a nutshell, they want to know what the other negotiator faces as a consequence if everyone fails to come to an agreement.

The BATNA is what is the best thing that they have available if the negotiation fails, and the WATNA is the worst thing. Knowing this can provide some serious leverage in a negotiation.

For example, if you know that the other negotiator is in a do-or-die position, you will be able to push them to the absolute limit before they will back out. If, on the other hand, this is an adverse situation and they have a variety of good offers on the table, then you will think twice before pushing too hard.

If the BATNA and WATNA are drastically different then it may change the game yet again. Perhaps the other negotiator was the one to make the offer, and has made the offer elsewhere, but none of those offers look like a "sure thing". Then the BATNA looks good, but the WATNA is complete failure. Then it gets interesting.

Then again, this strategy goes both ways, so in the end it really comes down to whose BATNA and WATNA are the best/worst and what they are willing to do to avoid going to Plan B.

Create loops.

Loops are a simple idea that come from hypnosis, and were famously used in the movie Inception in 2010. It is telling a story within a story to completely absorb the other person in your persuasive efforts.

For example, perhaps I tell you a story about a little girl who is exploring in the woods. After a while she decides to take a nap, and dreams of a huge library full of books and fairies. She follows the fairies to a magical room with a magical mirror. Inside that mirror she can see herself in a totally different world, filling with cake and presents and kids having fun!

She tries to touch the mirror but it shatters around her. She is disappointed that the cake and presents are gone, but that reminds her that it is time to leave the library.

Just then, she wakes up from her nap in the forest, gathers her belongings and runs home for dinner.

When you create a multi-levelled story, metaphor, or example, the listener has to work much harder to keep track of everything, and they tend to get consumed by the context-in-context. This technique is used in hypnosis and Behaviour Modification Therapy to create mental "distance" between the other person and the scenario they are imagining.

When coming "out" of the nested stories, each story has to be resolved in the reverse order that they began, so the first story is the last to finish. If stories are left unfinished it can leave the listener "hanging" and needing to know what happened, even if they don't realize you forgot to finish a story until later.

The most common example of this is when a friend is telling an anecdote from their day and they think of something urgent in the middle, and proceed to tell that story instead. If they forget to resume the original story, it feels unresolved because part of your short term memory is still working on it.

Elicit useful states.

Everybody's life has been full of memorable emotional experiences. Positive and negative. When we remember powerful experiences, some of the emotions associated with those experiences come back, and – to some degree – we relive the emotions all over again.

Eliciting a state is an idea from NLP, which is used to recall a memory with a useful emotion, and then use that emotion by attaching it to something new.

For example, if you had someone recall their favourite memory of their first love, and walk them through all the senses and details of the memory, you may be able to recall a very fond emotional state with it. This is a feeling and state of mind that anyone would enjoy.

If the other person is then made to imagine new things in connection with that old, good memory, the emotional feeling and the new stimuli become connected. Thereafter, every time the person thinks of the new thing – a thing that is helpful to the persuasion – they will experience some of the old positive emotions, and when you have such a positive connection with something, it is difficult not to want more of it.

Anchor emotions.

If possible, a best case scenario would be to recall that elicited state anytime you need it, which is exactly what anchoring is supposed to accomplish.

Imagine you have elicited this "first love" state in someone and they are mentally re-living that moment. Instead of connecting it to a new idea, you connect with a sugar packet (which just happens to be on the table). This would be done casually by saying something like "Ok, so if we use this sugar to represent that time in your life…" so the sugar becomes a physical metaphor for that feeling or experience.

The sugar then becomes a symbol for that feeling, the same way the number 6 is a symbol for any six items of any kind. By moving the sugar closer or farther away from that person their feeling increases or decreases, and by hiding and showing the sugar the feeling comes and goes.

From then on, that sugar packet, or any sugar packet that looks the same, represents a very positive emotional experience and it can be used or abused throughout a persuasion.

I once tried this with a stuffed animal at a party, and by the end of the party grown adults were fighting over it and carrying it around with them.

Manipulate symbols.

The "Octoberman Sequence" was something I found among the Pick-Up Artist community's lesser-known documentation, and it is supposedly banned among PUA's. It is a method of leading someone through visualizations, and it combines methods from hypnotism, seduction, and NLP to create and manipulate a symbol in someone's imagination. They consider it unethical because it can be so powerful. I can't fully do it justice here, but this is the gist:

You ask someone to imagine any positive emotion that you want to use. In the case of a PUA it is love, or love at first sight, or something similar. You "pace" every aspect of their body language from posture and body position to breathing and eye contact. The sequence is built to progressively increase bodily contact from nothing, to holding hands and onward, and the sky is the limit.

Once they have successfully imagined an emotion, and you have elicited a strong emotional state, you ask them to give the feeling some physical traits. For example, what colour is this emotion? Where do you feel it in your body? How big is it? What temperature is it? All the while matching their breathing, guiding their hands, etc.

Once this imaginary symbol has physical characteristics – all in their imagination – you begin manipulating the symbol. "Imagine it growing and shrinking as you breathe. You can feel it growing stronger with every breath, etc." The idea is to immerse them in a mental experience that you control, but that they have created. However, the real power comes when you take the symbol from them.

As the emotional object is rising and falling with each breath you tell them to imagine themselves breathing it out as they exhale and then the full-body sensation of breathing it in when they inhale. At some point, since you are matching their every movement, when they breath out, you breath it in, and "become" the symbol.

As you touch them they can feel it radiate from your finger across their skin and through their body ...and you can take it from there.

If done properly it supposedly creates an addiction to you, but I haven't confirmed that one for myself.

AVOID MANIPULATION

Manipulation has a weakness: the truth. Facts and figures can be checked. Logic can be analyzed. Be convinced by facts, not your feelings about the facts.

SUMMARY

Step 6 is about convincing and should be done after successfully completing the previous 5 steps.

Threshold:
Threshold is essentially the cost in time, money, effort, or required changes for a person to agree with the ultimate goal.

Progressive Explanation:
As we demonstrate our offer it is important to make it understandable. Progressive explanations allow someone to accept a big idea one small piece at a time, in a logical sequence.

Make it Engaging:
Persuasive rhythm ensures that a pattern never becomes repetitive enough to be boring. By combining progressive explanation and persuasive rhythm we get a completely engaging experience that is both understandable and entertaining.

The do-or-die moment in every persuasion is next: *Step 7: Close.* After successfully completing the 6 previous steps, closing can be much simpler than you may think. All we have to do then is resist the urge to persuade more.

STEP
07

Close

Ask confidently and simply. Then stop.

THE MOMENT OF TRUTH.

OR IS IT?

Of all the misunderstood elements of persuasion, nothing gets more hype than "closing" a deal. That is because – like all humans – we tend to focus on the moment of commitment, rather than everything that has built that decision from scratch.

A salesperson spends so much time preparing her knowledge, creating rapport, demonstrating and explaining a product or service, giving free trials, getting customer feedback, convincing with benefits and testimonials, and only after all of that persuasive effort, she asks the customer to make a purchase.

A movie shows us characters we love, creates a scenario to earn our sympathy, presents the characters with a challenge, we watch in anticipation as they struggle through obstacles, the tension mounts as they near their final goal, and only then are we fully emotionally committed to see them succeed or fail in the end.

After training, investigating, and responding to a call, police capture and disarm a criminal. The criminal is brought before an interrogator, who creates the emotional scenario to encourage a confession, earns the trust and credibility he needs, explains the criminal's options and benefits for confessing, and only after time, effort, and psychological tactics is the criminal in a position so desperate or comfortable that they are ready to document their confession on paper.

Even on a website, the agency plans and designs with the client to create a site that a customer will immediately trust and enjoy. The user likes what they see and experience on the site, they find things they need and begin the checkout process, and only after they have had a good experience with the site and entered all of their purchase information are they finally ready to click the "buy" button.

It takes 9 months for a baby to be born, not a few hours of labour. The same goes for persuasion.

(That was a metaphor – to clarify, very few persuasions take nine months, but all take longer than the *Close* step – see how smoothly metaphors make nonsense feel like facts?)

The perfect close is not a big event. It comes and goes as everyone expected, but without a lot of fanfare. After the close the persuader may celebrate with the other person and congratulate them on a great decision, but the close itself is just a close. The persuader is indifferent because they close all the time, remember?

Think of when you ask for insignificant things from people you've known for a long time. "Can you pass the salt, please?" Do you get nervous? Do you worry about whether they will say yes? Probably not. That's because it's something small and you are genuinely indifferent.

The salesperson closing the deal, the screenplay writer creating a climactic moment, the interrogator getting a confession, and the web agency making a website don't focus on whether the close is good or bad, they ensure that the entire process makes the close as likely as possible.

The best thing a persuader can do to increase the chances of a successful close is to change their attitude about what a close really is. It is not the make-or-break moment in a persuasion, and it is certainly not where you should focus your effort. A close is also not the "last chance" to convince the other person. It is the result of a good persuasion. A close fails due to a weak persuasion, not a weak close.

"Closing" is the yardstick of a persuasion, not the persuasion itself.

Blaming the close for a failure is like saying you were late because you walked through the door too slowly.

It can be very intimidating to ask someone for a big commitment, especially if it is your first time, or if the commitment is bigger than usual. One way or another it will be the end of the persuasion.

Well, not quite.

The previous 6 steps of Universal Persuasion are designed so they create an irresistible desire for the other person to commit or agree. Relatively often with these steps, the person being persuaded will ask to commit or agree before we even finish the whole sequence, removing the need to close at all.

When we close we are just allowing the person to finally become a part of the idea we have been pitching the whole time. The other person should want to seal the deal, we just have to let them.

When PUA's have done their jobs well, the girl is in eager anticipation of being asked for her phone number (a "number close"), a kiss (a "kiss close"), or more (the aforementioned "F-Close").

When a hostage negotiator has done their job perfectly the criminal is left without negotiating power, hostages, or options, and they want to give up.

When a cult leader asks a person to join their movement that person finds it hard to imagine their lives without their new-found belief system.

When the military asks a soldier to risk their lives for the sake of their country, saying no would mean giving up their entire lifestyle and everything they have worked so hard to achieve (not to mention the consequences of a court-martial).

When McDonald's asks us to pay, we are so close to satisfying our hunger we gladly hand over the cash, and (too) often we Supersize it!

When an interrogator asks a criminal to confess, the criminal is so relieved to get it off their chest or so afraid of the consequences of not cooperating, they volunteer. In actuality, if the criminal doesn't willingly co-operate a confession isn't legally acceptable.

When a customer wants to complete an online purchase, they are already looking for the "buy" button.

REDUCE FRICTION: GIVE THEM A PEN

Although we may have convinced someone to commit to something huge, actually saying "yes" is a very easy thing to do. Whether they have to sign a contract, reveal a phone number, or trade money for a product, it usually only takes a minute or two. Even an extensive contract-signing escapade happens in a single meeting. The main thing the persuader must do is provide them with whatever they need to do it now.

There is a fragility during a close – for the person being persuaded – of which most people (including persuaders) become aware in that moment, and that is why a close can be nerve-wracking. The other person suddenly becomes aware that they are committing to something and if it is stretched out for too long or becomes too awkward, they can get "cold feet" like so many nervous grooms. Our job is to prevent that from happening.

If they are signing the contract, hand them the contract and a pen. If they are giving their number, hand them your phone, ready for input. If they are paying, just hold out your hand and tell them the amount. Whatever it happens to be, make it easy. Insurance salespeople are famous for having all the necessary forms with them at any given moment. This is not the time to provide unnecessary resistance.

ACT WITH VALUE

It is absolutely necessary to act as if you are assuming they will agree, expecting them to agree, and ready for them to agree. All salespeople everywhere have heard that you should "assume the sale" and that is excellent advice. Don't think, just do.

Have you ever questioned a person at a restaurant for asking you to pay? Technically that is when they are closing, but we never give it a second thought. Neither do they, for that matter. Most often they say "thank you", hand you the bill, and walk away. Now that's an assumptive close!

It's because they assume you will pay. I once had a new retail employee tell me the amount I had to pay as if she thought it was really expensive, and it was the only time I ever second-guessed a purchase while standing at the cash register. My first thought was "hmm... maybe that *is* a little expensive."

A DIFFICULT CLOSE

The idea of making it easy for people to agree becomes vitally important in situations where it is actually quite a lot of effort to formally commit. Politicians often have this problem when a large percentage of voters just don't vote at all, and it is probably true that elections would sometimes have different winners if everyone had turned out to vote.

I once read a story of a mayoral candidate who had strong support among the inner city population, who were poor, lived quite far from the polling station, and therefore had a poor history of voter turn-out. When election time came the candidate literally took carloads of people – who were eager to vote – to and from the polls, and he eventually won the election by a narrow margin.

In cases like this a persuader must brainstorm ways to make it easier to vote. A close doesn't need convincing per se but be aware that friction or threshold might be the only barrier to success. Provide information, reduce the effort, complete some of the process for people when possible and – worst case scenario – put them in your car and drive them to the polling station. Rather than just handing the contract over, point to the line and say "sign here, please". No thinking required.

EMPTY CLOSING

On some occasions the person we are trying to close may provide what PUA's call "last minute resistance". The person may have a sudden moment of uncertainty or hesitation about closing.

In these situations almost everyone's immediate response is to give one last push to convince, assuming the other person is 99% convinced already. This is the worst possible strategy during that crucial moment, because the problem isn't the convincing, it's the persuader.

In persuasion there is never a reason to go back a step (unless you start a new persuasion). If the persuader is still convincing, they aren't closing. By pushing harder, the persuader suddenly drops their value (it seems like they're begging or worried), they start adding arguments to their rational thinking (which only decreases their emotional thinking), and they take a step back to convincing rather than trying to close.

The solution is an "empty close".

In a movie, this is when we think the hero has died and all hope is lost. In a pick-up it is when the woman has a moment of rational concern before "committing" with the PUA. In interrogation the criminal may question his actions while writing the confession. The groom has one little moment of regret about not being a bachelor anymore.

Just when we thought the hero has died, we begin hoping he isn't really dead. When the woman has second thoughts, the PUA agrees, turns on the lights, and says that when a girl says no, he never takes advantage of her. When the criminal hesitates to confess, the police threaten to take away their deal. When the groom worries, the Best Man says "if you don't go through with this, does that mean I can ask her out?"

Instead of pushing harder, we completely pull back and stop *allowing* them to close. We wouldn't take the contract and pen away though. The trick is to keep it as easy as possible to turn the persuader around.

The persuader can also "future pace" them, which means to follow their logic through into the future. If they decide not to agree now, they will face the same need they have now, but they won't have our solution anymore. But the most important thing to us is that they get what they need, whether it is us or someone else.

Resistance is almost always based on the other person having second thoughts about the person who has just persuaded them. It is sort of like realizing "I am about to let myself be persuaded to do this, is this really someone I want to allow to get me like this?" If we push harder it confirms that we are only after selfish goals, but if we seem helpful, appreciative, and ready to pull away, it shows that we are putting them first and that we are not trying to be manipulative. Sometimes this can even mean that we give some supporting arguments for the "other option" as a way to show that we are not saying the other choice is bad, just that our choice is better.

When executed properly, this technique can be shockingly effective. The hero comes back and succeeds beyond all expectations.

THEN, STOP

After closing successfully a persuader feels on top of their game. Creating a masterful persuasion is very satisfying and will make the persuader want to repeat that mastery again and again – and they should – just not right away.

If the other person can offer the persuader multiple victories over time, or if the persuader has made sacrifices to get to this successful moment, it can feel almost irresistible to add or revisit those requests during their triumphant moment.

Remember that all people want to maximize their motivational gains. In this moment of success the persuader will feel tempted to make it continue or take advantage of the success to get more success.

This can create an instant feeling of resentment for the other person (the feeling that they are being "milked") or can create an overload, since the persuader hasn't completed the 6 steps toward this new and unexpected "second close".

At McDonald's we are asked to Supersize before we pay, because we are still in process of choosing. If we paid first and then we were offered to Supersize it would feel like a second purchase, and very few people would agree.

If you're thinking "but I have always been taught to up-sell, and sometimes it works!" that is true. But the only effective up-sell is one that is built into the process of convincing and closing, not one that comes after the close is complete.

In a retail environment we are often asked to become a "member" of their in-house discount program, or we are told about extra items that are on sale. At the grocery store the chocolate bars and gum are just before the checkout, not after. A proper up-sell happens just as the close is about to happen, so at the absolute climax of the persuasion something else might sneak through as well.

After the close, stop.

To up-sell effectively it has to be a part of the original deal. Sometimes we can make the original offer an up-sell (buy two, get one free!) so that the person can "down-sell" us instead. If they buy two, that's twice the profit, if they buy one, they still bought one. Either way, we win.

There is one type of scenario that looks like an exception to this idea, but it isn't: Superfluous details.

When designing online registration forms, marketing departments often try to sneak in some extra questions that aren't required for registration, but are useful information, like asking for age or gender.

In theory it seems like adding them to the original form as an "upsell" is the best way to get that information. In practice, more people answer those questions if they are asked after the transaction is complete.

The confusion happens because for the marketers the form itself feels like the prize. For the person registering, the form is merely an obstacle on the way to the prize. More questions creates more friction.

When those extra questions are treated as a separate persuasion, suddenly the completion rate improves.

TRY THIS AT HOME

Your mission, should you choose to accept it, is to ask for things you want more often. If you are a beginner to persuasion, you literally just have to practice asking confidently.

And remember, you're not asking permission, you're asking for a commitment from the other person. There is a difference.

Every time you want anything, for the next few weeks, ask for it. If you're in a restaurant and you want a slight variation of something from the menu, ask for it. If there is someone you want a date with, ask for it. If someone has been treating you badly or taking advantage of you, ask them to stop and smile while you do it.

For non-beginners – especially if you work with people for a living – there is a good chance that you actually have to practice saying "no" before you ask for what you want. Tell your customer "no, that deadline is too tight" and ask them to sign the contract anyway, with a smile. You will be happy to finish it by a more realistic deadline instead.

Tell your spouse "no, I would rather not go to that place for dinner" and then suggest the option you really want instead, confidently, with a smile.

Sometimes we want to close so badly that we will agree to any last-minute request from the other person and regret it later. We might even get praise for catering to the client's every request, but a close has to benefit the persuader too!

If you are afraid of the other person, or if you are worried that they might say no, *they are persuading you*, not the other way around.

Open a conversation, create rapport, isolate the other person, explain why you want what you want, and then close!

When they say yes, stop! Then bask in the glory of your success.

AVOID MANIPULATION

To avoid manipulation, one would hope that you have escaped before the moment of the close. By this time you're in pretty deep, but you aren't committed until you are committed. Despite overwhelming pressure you can always say "no".

It would be nice to say that someone who tries "too hard" to get a close is being manipulative, but in reality most people try too hard, so don't take it as a sign of anything, necessarily.

A persuader's reaction to a failure can say a lot about what it means for the persuader. Typically it means they will make less money, or their ego has taken a hit. That's normal, and the result will be disappointment, surprise, or even a little spitefulness because they have worked hard, only to fail. However, a persuader should be trying to keep everything positive or at least civil, because the relationship should continue into the future.

It can be worth faking some last minute resistance to see how the persuader handles it. If they get threatening or furious, or if the reaction is more like fear rather that insecurity or disappointment it could indicate that they have something to lose.

Nobody is genuinely afraid or extremely angry just because something didn't work out. At best it indicates that they would make a terrible person to be involved with, but at worst it might mean that there are consquences for them because you are saying no. Con artists or criminals often risk something to try to persuade us, so failure means they will have to answer to someone else or absorb a loss.

But don't jump to conclusions. Communicate! Tell them you're hesitant and ask why they are reacting like they are. When faced with explaining they may reveal that this is a big deal for them and they had to say no other prospects to pursue it. Or they might get defensive and refuse an explanation.

If you have doubts, or if you are prone to impulse decisions, take a break before closing. Put your mind into something else to clear out your purely emotional decision-making. Now would be a perfect time to get a second opinion.

If reducing friction is the best way to get a quick close, give yourself some extra friction to see if it changes your mind. Are you only closing because it's so easy, or because you really want it? Addictive or pleasurable activities often lose some of their charm when extra effort is required. You may really want that chocolate when it's in your cabinet, 5 feet away, but if you have to walk to the store to get it, are you still interested?

SUMMARY

Just ask, and give them a pen.
Do it confidently and provide the means for the other person to agree right here, right now. Otherwise, if you're asking, you're closing.

Empty Close
If there is any last minute resistance, back off and release the pressure rather than adding more. "It's a big decision, take your time." Maintain your value.

Then, stop!
When you have successfully closed, resist the temptation to think this is the time to take care of other things you want. There is a time

and a place for everything, but only one persuasion at a time, please!

Once the deal is done the interaction may be over, but the persuasion isn't. In the next step we will build a memory of the persuasion that they will enjoy and defend, forever.

STEP
08

Summarize
With Bias

Review everything and emphasize the positives.

WHAT IF NOTHING YOU REMEMBERED WAS TRUE?

Actually, not a single anecdotal memory in your head is accurate. The memory of your life is a combination of what really happened, what you believe happened, and everything you have learned and experienced since then.

Memory is not a video that we can replay. There are things that we are absolutely sure we remember exactly the way they happened, but we don't. There are pieces missing, details that have changed, and events that – if you were really pressed to describe – your mind would invent out of thin air.

Anyone who watches reality television knows that while an outside observer will see a situation happen one way, the people in that situation can come out of it with very different renditions of the events that transpired; even from each other.

Dating is the classic example: one person thinks it went well, only to receive a "thanks, but no thanks" call/email/text the next day.

Yet again, intuition fails us. It's difficult to accept, I know.

Once we accept it, however, a whole range of possibilities open before us, because if your head is full of partially-correct memories, so are everyone else's. And if everyone makes inaccurate memories for themselves, persuaders can – and do – make some for them as well.

The beautiful part is, no one can tell the difference between what they remember correctly and what they remember incorrectly.

Human memory is both a fascinating predictive tool, and a minefield of flaws. Using a few simple techniques at the end of the persuasion, a persuader can make sure the other person remembers the persuasion as something positive that they want to continually be a part of. In terms of the 3-step model of convincing we discussed before, this is the "tell them what you told them" step.

We like to think that when we remember an event that the memory is pretty close to the way it happened. That is almost never true. Our memories are actually very flexible, and as a persuader it can be a big advantage if someone remembers an interaction as something they would like to repeat.

More importantly, the worst thing that can happen to a persuasion is that the other person regrets being persuaded. This is why stores have a return policy or an "all sales are final" policy, depending on the shelf-life of their products.

It happens relatively often that a person will regret an emotional decision after giving it some rational consideration (and by "rational consideration" I mean they experience a motivational loss because of their decision). This is called "Buyer's Remorse". Using a few simple tactics a persuader can not only avoid negative aftershocks, but can make the persuasion self-affirming, forever.

END ON A HIGH NOTE

It is a simple and invaluable piece of advice, and you've probably heard it before: end with positive emotions. Whether it's a blockbuster movie or a one-night-stand or a business deal with an important CEO, the last impression is more important than the "first impression". Comedians and fortune tellers alike always try to make the last thing they say the best thing they say.

If a persuader can genuinely send the other person home when they're having fun, it is likely that they will remember the whole persuasion as a fun experience. As we learned before, the best positive emotion is a gain in motivational goals.

Another common piece of advice is "leave them wanting more." That is precisely what we're getting at here. Try to recognize when the persuasion is over and everyone is feeling great and take that as an opportunity to say goodbye.

A persuader should make the other person feel like it was nice to meet them (rather than just saying it), make reference to something funny that was said during their time together, or future-pace to create anticipation for all the great things that will happen now that agreement has happened. "We're really excited to have you on board, this can only bring prosperity to us both."

Really listening to someone during an interaction should provide many examples of positive things to re-visit in the final moments of the persuasion.

Regardless of the method, let them leave with a smile on their face and an optimistic attitude.

SUMMARIZE WITH BIAS

During any interaction there will be aspects that move the persuasion forward as well as aspects that provide some resistance or even disagreement. Even the most persuasive salesman will have to overcome objections and apprehensions. At the end of the interaction, whether or not it went well, we should always re-state the preceding events in a way that emphasizes the positive, effective points. By summarizing with bias we not only shift the favour toward our own goals, we help the other person feel that they have made the right choice. Our choice.

From day-to-day gossip to historical events, everyone summarizes with bias. It's the winners of wars that write history, not the losers.

The ultimate example of a summarizing with bias has to be The Bible, believed by roughly 2.1 billion Christians worldwide, counting all the ones that haven't been to church for years *(Affiliation)*.

Whether or not The Bible is the word of God, it was edited and compiled by humans, just as it is edited, re-written, translated and re-printed by humans today ("Simple English" version, anyone?). Originally it was edited to create political and social power, with no intention of being truthful or complete. At the time, church and government were almost the same thing, and the ruling powers chose to supplement their power with religious documents.

When The Bible was canonized during the first few centuries A.D., books were included or ignored based on the decisions of bishops, priests, and rulers of the time.

There were actually several versions of Christian culture, including the Egyptians, Hebrews, Babylonians, and Ethiopians. Each of these versions, especially the Ethiopian version, included or excluded biblical books of their own choosing even when those texts were forbidden by others. Although we are given the impression that The Bible consists of certain gospels, handed down from generation to generation, it was literally libraries worth of writings that were passed on. And not all of those books told the same stories.

The books and stories that were included in The Bible were those that were most religiously acceptable, most beautifully written, and that united the community.

I.e. – the positive aspects were emphasized.

On the other hand, those that were not chosen were the books that went against the majority, created difficult questions, or gave the power of worship to individuals rather than the church.

I.e. – the negative aspects were removed and forgotten.

Keeping in mind that the Church of the time was equal to, or stronger than the government of the time, these would have been very significant choices.

Some of the excluded books contained stories of Adam's first wife Lilith, Mary's other kids, angels violating women, Hell being a nice place, and Jesus resurrecting a friend for his own gain. Needless to say, those stories would have caused quite a dilemma for the religious leaders of the time.

Because of summarizing with bias, Christianity was changed forever and is now followed by about 30% of the world, and the excluded stories are long forgotten by most people.

Although it won't be nearly as dramatic when a typical persuader summarizes with bias, it works on the same principle. The persuader just has to quickly review what happened during the persuasion, leaving out all the bad parts. The other person will remember the new, more positive version instead.

If we were to walk into a store to buy furniture, we may be disappointed in several options before finally choosing one and being persuaded to buy a warranty on our purchase. However, when the sales person reviews what we're about to buy he may phrase it like "We are going with the genuine Italian leather sofa, with the chaise longue option and manufacturer-guaranteed quality for 20 years. This was an excellent choice. You will enjoy this sofa for a long time." What he left out was that it was smaller than we wanted, more expensive than we wanted, and that the guarantee was an extra $300. When we tell our friends about it though, we will highlight all the things he said and may not even remember what we were looking for when we walked into the store.

Repeating the positive or useful elements of a conversation, especially when the other person brought them up, allows the persuader to influence what the other person remembers. In the same way that history books are always written from the point of view of the winners, you will prescribe memories from your own point of view, which also happens to be flattering for the other person.

A comedian ends with his best joke and we are still laughing at it the next day. We re-live the experience with our friends when the best jokes become a meme in our lives. We seem to forget all the mediocre jokes.

The way a movie ends can change our entire experience. We have spent most of the movie living vicariously through the main characters, so when they succeed we feel as if we have succeeded. The most cunning screenplays make us enjoy the un-happy ending, but this is difficult to do in any other persuasion. The sad ending is more of a "special case"; the highest grossing movies tend to have very happy, very satisfying endings that leave us energized. Even the writers of Titanic created a parallel storyline with a happy ending, rather than leave it as a tragedy.

A popular form of entertainment is the highlight reel where we are only shown the greatest moments from a career, a life, a sports season, etc.

Summarizing an interaction may sound like an awkward thing to do, but in most cases it is not only comfortable and natural, people appreciate that you were paying attention. In business meetings most people actually prefer for it to be done, and sometimes done again in an email, so that everybody is on the same page.

USE FALSE MEMORY

Sometimes our memories are just wrong, but until proven wrong, they feel right. The simplest example is numbers. Statistics can change within one meeting. Even though the presentation said "36%" a person may remember 38%, or 63%, or even a totally unrelated number when they re-tell it to someone else later.

That is why advertising and news often use phrases like "Over 3000 people" rather than "3129 people", because 3000 is easier to remember. An ad might say "almost 80% of people choose this product" or list the price as $4.99. Although technically truthful, through word-of-mouth the numbers change to 80% and $4 because it's simpler.

Many studies have been done on false memories. For example, adults can be told 5 stories about their childhood; 4 are true and one is a completely false story about getting lost at the mall when they were a young child. When interviewed later, they will recall all five stories equally well, and when told one is false, many people will believe it was one of the true stories, because they all *feel* the same.

People may alter a memory after-the-fact, based on new thoughts and ideas they have had. We always recall old experienced based on our current information, and it is fairly common to mix up thoughts that occurred during the interaction and those that happened afterward.

In a book called *Remembering*, by F.C. Bartlett, he conducted a series of experiments where "average" people were told stories from cultures very different from their own. They were then asked to repeat the stories a few hours, days, or even months later, and the differences between their version and the original were analyzed.

Without exception, every person modified the stories to fill in the parts they couldn't remember clearly, change details, etc., and modifications generally adapted things they were unfamiliar with to fit their own experience. In other words, when the memory was fuzzy, they added something familiar. Several weeks later many of the new versions barely resembled the original story at all. This was true with stories, images, and symbols recalled from memory.

We can amplify the good aspects of what happened – especially if they are complimentary to the other person – to an almost ridiculous level before someone will question the accuracy of the statement. For example, if you tell someone that they are a shrewd negotiator, or even funnier than you expected them to be, or that they care a lot about their family and you respect that in a person, it is very unlikely that they will disagree. In this step, the self-delusion we learned in Step 2 is a very powerful tool.

Furthermore, if they change their request to be better than their original request all you have to do is confirm it. If they originally ordered 10 units and they say "So when will those 20 units be delivered?" All we have to do is say "I can deliver 20 units by Friday. Can we confirm that order now?" If they confirm, just do the paperwork and proceed as usual. They may have thought in the meantime that 20 would have been better than 10, and subconsciously changed the memory of the deal to match it.

Another excellent use of false memories is when a persuader sets up the other person with everything they need to come up with an idea "on their own". Five minutes later the other person will have no memory of the persuader presenting 90% of the idea; they will only remember the last 10% that was their own creative genius.

You may think that changes like this only happen in a perfect world, but they happen all the time. In subjective fields especially, details are changed regularly, and specifications are often written after the persuasion, including inaccurate details. The finer points like exact numbers and deadlines are often not included in the original contracts.

Fortune Tellers make their living by creating false memories and summarizing with bias, using linguistic acrobatics. Even though they will begin with a statement like "I am seeing an address, it includes the number 4, does that make sense?" After the customer elaborates, giving information about the summer cottage with that address and the neighbor that lived next door the fortune teller will summarize at the end with "Ok, so I saw your summer cottage, with the address 604, and you and your neighbor playing tag in the yard."

Shockingly, that is how the customer will remember it as well. This is how psychics and the like have become a multi-million dollar industry, and have existed for hundreds of years.

CREATE A VICIOUS CYCLE

The most brilliant way to affect a person's impression of a persuasion after-the-fact is to create a vicious cycle that re-enforces the belief that the other person has made a great decision (which they are inclined to believe anyway).

Religions generally have a component within the belief system that says anyone outside that belief system needs to be saved, or educated, or is unworthy in God's eyes *(Status, Affiliation, Justice)*. Believers are taught that criticism from non-believers is the proof that the non-believer must be saved, and anything a believer can do to help them is what a good believer should do. It is probably the most brilliant aspect of religious beliefs, and I must admit, I admire its persuasive affect.

Think about this for a second: beliefs like that create a persuasion that never ends. It not only eliminates Buyer's Remorse, it is a self-sustaining cycle without any need for the original persuader. Moreover, it creates the motivation to spread the persuasion to any person who doesn't already believe in it *(Status, Affiliation)*.

A simpler, more common version of a vicious cycle is to blame "jealousy" for any criticisms. This is one of the ways people tend to rationalize their own actions when they are met with disapproval. "They only hate me because they're jealous of my success. I am proud of what I've done and they should be ashamed of themselves for being jealous." Instead of realizing they might be at fault, they are convinced that the other person's jealousy justifies their action, and they might believe that forever. It creates a neat little package of a biased summary (forget the damage, be proud!), a motivational gain (well done, me!), and a vicious cycle (anyone else who disagrees with me is also jealous).

Creating a certification process is another cunning way to make people work towards a purchase, over and over. If an organization can "certify" people *(Status)* to use their own product or service, then it means that the company selling the product or service is also able to make people de-certified by updating the product! A new version of the product means a new certification is required. An expiry date on the certification means they have to continually train and learn the product until they switch to another product or choose a new profession. It's so simple, yet so effective, and nobody ever stops to ask why they need to be certified in the first place.

TRY THIS AT HOME

This is an easy step to understand, and a little practice can improve how smoothly we use summarization in a conversation.

Choose any event that has been witnessed by someone else too. It could be as simple as a television episode you have both watched. Tell this person you want to practice summarizing things and re-tell the events of the episode, only including the best parts.

Then ask if they agree with your summarization. If they do, great! If they don't, pay attention to what they think you left out. It is possible that some negative events are necessary to the plot line, but ultimately the ending should be happy and satisfying.

For more advanced practice, try taking a situation that seems negative and explaining it like it has a "silver lining". Look for the good in the bad. If you can make someone else say "Hmmm, that's true. I hadn't looked at it like that," you have succeeded.

AVOID MANIPULATION

To avoid manipulation after a persuasion you will need your thinking cap.

Everything in this step is a matter of using our natural cognitive biases and intuition against us, and it is very easy to fall for it.

Technically, if someone has come this far in manipulating you, you may have already committed to something without realizing it was a bad decision. Your immediate concern should be to undo that bad decision, but in this step we are also trying to avoid continuing to repeat that mistake, or pass it on to others.

Summarizing with bias can make you feel as if something in which you have been a part was all of the good and none of the bad that actually happened. If your actions or decisions will hurt you, cost you, or put you in some risk, that's not persuasion. If you will gain and other people will experience hurt, cost or risk, that isn't persuasion either.

Damaging behaviour —when added to a vicious cycle – can create long-term threats to your health and well-being. Anorexia for example, is a vicious cycle built from the belief that *not* eating makes you more attractive, and eating makes you less attractive. That is a *false dichotomy*, because eating is not the opposite of being attractive. What makes people attractive is being healthy, which entails eating the right amount. But since many people eat too much, it gives the illusion that food-wise less is more.

This type of vicious cycle, once entered, has very damaging psychological effects that are hard to break and hard to recover from. It can even lead to addiction.

People and organizations that benefit from negative vicious cycles will usually use strong isolation as a key method to maintain their cycles. The less you know and the less you think, the better for them. A vicious cycle is, in effect, permanent social isolation, maintained by you. Beware of answers that are too broad and vague to address your questions, and beware when you ask about other possibilities and are shamed or dismissed for your curiosity.

An abusive relationship is another type of vicious cycle. If you are in a relationship like that you might believe that nobody else could ever want you because *the abusive person* thinks you are crap. This makes you cling to the abusive person as your last hope. It is a vicious cycle. They decide when you fail, only they have the power to fix it, and they set up impossible expectations so you can fail again. But *you* are the one who feels unworthy, which makes you believe nobody would want you, and the whole thing starts again.

Beware of any scenario where your only option is to fail and be forgiven. Especially if failure is unavoidable. Forgiveness brings you back to zero; it is not a benefit. If you must continually be forgiven just so you remain eligible for a reward that you might never actually achieve, you are in a vicious cycle.

If you have ever asked God's forgiveness so you will be allowed into heaven, you might be closer to this than it seems.

Think for yourself, then ask questions, then think some more. It is your best defense. Everyone acts out of self-interest all the time, so if the "powerful" people aren't getting anything out of the arrangement, why are they so interested in you?

SUMMARY

Persuaders can use the flaws of human memory to their advantage, and it will go totally undetected.

End on a High Note:
By ending every persuasion with positive emotions, it will create a lasting impression of positivity, regardless of how the persuasion actually transpired.

Summarize with Bias:
At the end of a persuasion a persuader can summarize with bias by re-iterating the interaction like a highlight reel of the positive, effective elements of the experience. Doing this will have a strong influence on the way the other person remembers the persuasion and how they will re-tell it to other people.

Use False Memory:
False memory gives us the ability to supply someone with memories that didn't actually happen. Whether we compliment them on actions they didn't actually do (actions that help us), traits they don't actually have (traits that help us), or confirm details that have changed (details that help us), it can be very useful.

Create a Vicious Cycle:
A Vicious Cycle allows a persuasion to continue motivating a person and re-establishing their belief in the persuasion forever, without any further input from the persuader. If the persuader is also able to gather their believers once a week to be re-committed, that helps too.

Conclusion

& Bibliography

Now that you have learned all 8 steps, and the ingredients of effective persuasion, I would like to share some final thoughts and suggestions for readers that are interested in learning more.

You have come a long way since the stories about Titanic, John's military career, and Juan Mann's Free Hugs Campaign!

Undoubtedly many of the persuasive steps discussed throughout this book felt familiar, and you can probably think of times when you have done them intuitively. Now that you understand the mechanics of each step, perhaps – with a little fine tuning – your intuitive method will become a powerful method for all of the persuasive situations in your life.

There is a certain symmetry (or perhaps irony) in writing a book about persuasion because the book itself must be persuasive. If you are reading this chapter, it would appear that the persuasion of the book was a success. If you found the book entertaining and helpful, then it was definitely successful. The goal of a book is, after all, to be readable, engaging, and informative.

The more you know about persuasion the more you will begin to realize that persuasion happens to us everyday. You will see yourself being persuaded and you may have mixed feelings about it. On the one hand you'll be noticing the things you have learned – as they happen – which makes you a more effective, observant person. On the other hand, you will be tempted to disagree with things that are good for you, merely because it is hard to "let yourself" be persuaded *(Status)*.

The same was true of this book itself. Most authors use the Preface at the beginning of the book to explain their intentions and give insight about how the book was written, but in this book that would have required making you, the reader, aware of being persuaded about persuasion. Complicated, indeed.

Now that you understand the mechanics of persuasion you can understand that persuasion is necessary in any book, and why I left a little of the book's "transparency" until the end.

This book has been built on the 8 Universal Steps of Persuasion, in two levels. The chapters of the book have been structured based on the 8 Universal Steps themselves. This makes the steps and process easier to remember and also allows you to easily use this book as a reference in the future.

The second level of persuasion is that the whole book was a persuasion as well. In addition to teaching the 8 Universal Steps, hopefully the book can be a good example of those steps in and of itself.

Each chapter was treated as a small persuasion of its own, and followed the format of the 8 steps. It Opened & Disarmed with uniquely-designed title pages, dramatic opening statements, and a quick explanation of what you would learn. If you had stopped reading after the opening statement (in huge type, no less) you would have remained curious about what you were missing.

Then it was important to give some easy, familiar examples and make sure that every reader understood the basic concept, regardless of experience. To get more information you merely had to keep reading, so the "turn around" was built in.

In the persuasion of a book the Isolation step is rather difficult, because I can't control where you read. But there is also the matter of allowing you to focus on the material being presented. In some chapters it was necessary to explain alternative ideas that exist in the world so you could decide what you think and move on to the rest of the chapter.

The convincing part of each chapter was when you read about how each step actually works, and learned the components, in progressive baby steps.

After learning why it is important and how it works, it was time to Close, which was the *Try This At Home* section and *Avoid Manipulation* section of each chapter. Some readers want to be more persuasive, while other readers want to be manipulated less, so both serve as a close depending on your goals. In person I would have only presented one or the other.

Then we summarized each chapter to make it easier to remember and refer to in the future.

In the persuasion of the book in general, the steps are a lot like the movie studio persuading us to see a movie. In this case the reader is the audience, and the persuasion begins before you start reading the book.

If you bought this book on Amazon.com, you had to read the description, maybe some reviews, and judge it from the design. If you borrowed it from a friend, their opinion and the physical book itself helped you decide to start reading.

The most common questions I got while writing this book were "what is it about?" and "how many pages will it be?" Everyone was trying to decide if it was easy enough to get through. I got the hint. During editing, over 100 pages were removed from the original, and the design itself was made to feel informal and easy-to-read.

I used stories to introduce persuasion instead of diving into the details, so it felt easier. Then we built on those stories to learn about each of the 8 steps.

Throughout the rest of the book you learned progressively,

one step at a time. Step 6 also included Tips & Tricks, which were different than other chapters and helped break the pattern of the book overall.

The *Close* of the overall book was to demonstrate that all persuasion and manipulation are built on the same ingredients, and – like a movie – to leave you feeling satisfied and inspired.

And now, after all that, you have arrived at this chapter, which is just about to finish summarizing the whole book with bias.

You may be left with some questions after realizing that the method being described was being used the whole time.

Did I present myself as a reluctant author just because it's true or am I using the composite method of creating a reluctant "hero" like Neil Strauss did to himself in his best-selling book, *The Game*?

Did you like the stories in the introduction because they are interesting stories, or because they were written using the 8 Steps?

In Step 5, did I say "Focus. This is important." because it was particularly important, or because your focus created figurative isolation? And why didn't I use the word "focus" for the rest of the chapter?

Did I really use quotes throughout the book because they "break the pattern" or because they are one of the sneaky methods described in Step 6? Maybe both! How many other methods from Step 6 did I use?

Did I purposely skip the dramatic opening of this chapter and make the intro text boring and uninformative so nobody would read it first and spoil the book?

And how many other tricks am I not telling you about?

You may never know.

FURTHER READING

If I have persuaded you to do one thing, it was to keep reading; otherwise you wouldn't be reading this. And if you have read this far, you are aware of exactly how I persuaded you.

First and foremost, I appreciate your attention very much, and I would be happy to have you as a visitor on my persuasion blog, **www.thehipperelement.com.**

However, now you might be interested in some of the books and sites that were used in the creation of this book. It would have been impossible to include all the details from all of the disciplines included in this research, so here you will find a small, selected bibliography of books that were most interesting, useful, or surprising. They all contributed to this book, even if that contribution was to eliminate a possible approach from the overall method.

In addition to these references I can also recommend Wikipedia, www.mindhacks.com, and www.sciencedaily.com in general.

Ariely, Dan. (2010). *Predictably Irrational: The Hidden Forces That Shape Our Decisions.* New York: Harper-Collins.

This book is very easy to read and tackles one major aspect of our seemingly irrational behavior in each chapter. Ariely created and performed experiments that demonstrate these behaviors in predictable ways.

Bandler, Richard & Grinder, John. (1975). *Patterns of the Hypnotic Technique of Milton H. Erikson, M.D.* Scotts Valley: Grinder & Associates.

One of the early influences on NLP, Bandler and Grinder breakdown the patterns of one of the most successful hypnotists ever to practice professionally.

Barone, David F., & Hersen, Michel, & Hasselt, Vincent Van
B. (Eds.). (2003). *Advanced Personality*. New York:
Plenum Press.
This is a graduate-level text that provides an academic overview
of many personality theories and research done in each case.

Bartlett, Sir Frederic C. (1995). *Remembering: A Study in
Experimental and Social Psychology*. Cambridge:
Cambridge Univeristy Press
This book re-tells a series of experiments that presented stories
and images to people and then asked them to recall those items later,
keeping track of the differences in memories.

Campbell, Joseph. (1993). *The Hero With A Thousand Faces*.
London, FontanaPress.
This is a rather heavy, academic book that brilliantly de-codes
mythology into a single, reliable formula. Many major movies and
books have been influenced by this book since its publication,
including Star Wars and The Matrix.

Carter, Rita. (2009) *The Human Brain Book*. London:
Dorling Kindersley.
On the surface this book appears to be a picture book about
the brain, but in actuality it is a brilliantly simple presentation of
neuroscience basics, which I would recommend to anyone of any age.
All textbooks should be done like this book.

Ekman, Paul. (2003). *Emotions Revealed: Recognizing Faces
and Feelings to Improve Communication and
Emotional Life*. New York: Holt.
Ekman makes the complicated subject of facial expressions
interesting and accessible.

Givens, David, B. (2002). *The Non-Verbal Dictionary of Gestures, Signs & Body Language Cues*. Spokane: Center for Nonverbal Studies.

The title says it all. What this book lacks in engagement and presentation, it makes up in thoroughness.

Greene, Robert. (2006). *The 48 Laws of Power*. London: Profile Books.

The new machiavellian bible. This book simplifies centuries of manipulative history into 48 basic rules for controlling the people around you.

Godwin, Maurice Grover. (2001). *Criminal Psychology and Forensic Technology*. Boca Raton: CRC Press.

Not the most warm and friendly book, but good if you want to get an overview of the serious side of interrogation approaches and methods.

Gudjonsson, Gisli H. (2003). *The Psychology of Interrogations and Confessions*. London: Wiley

This book examines, in a fairly academic manner, the pros and cons of techniques that produce confessions. It specifically deals with the weakness of producing false confessions.

Hall, Michael L. (2005) *Figuring Out People, Reading People Using Meta-Programs*. Clifton: Neuro-Semantic Publications.

You could say that this book provides a more complicated, but more considered style of personality typology through detailed traits and a comprehensive list of NLP-focused profiling. The goal of the book was to be comprehensive, rather than practical.

Hawkins, Jeff & Blakeslee, Sandra. (2004). *On Intelligence*. New York: St. Martin's Griffin.

Spectacular book about the way Hawkins believes the human brain works and how it might be used to make intelligent machines in the future. His discussion about how people process information was a new, fantastic point of view.

Ignatius, Adi (Ed.). (2011, Spring) *Hardvard Business Review OnPoint, Selected Articles from HBR*. Whole issue.
Good magazine, and this particular issue was dedicated completely to persuasion and influence, especially when we are not the one in an official position of power.

Jablonka, Eva & Lamb, Marion J. (2006). *Evolution in Four Dimensions*. Cambridge: MIT Press.
Includes interesting discussion about behavior as a factor in general evolution.

Lidwell, William, & Holden, Kritina & Butler, Jill. (2003). *Universal Principles of Design*. Beverly: Rockport.
This book collects 100 principles for designing anything so it works well with the way people perceive, interpret, and understand.

Keirsey, David. (1998). *Please Understand Me II*. Del Mar: Prometheus.
One of the most popular books about personality types, it provides typology for many major aspects of life. Although I disagree with typology in general, it was a good reference for what type of information is easy and popular to believe.

Knepper, Kenton & Tank, J. (Unknown). *Completely Cold*. No publisher info.
A 30-page book that explains a quick-and-dirty method for giving readings in a fortune-telling context.

Kroeger, Otto, & Thuesen, Janet M. (1988). *Type Talk, The 16*

*Personality Types That Determine How We Live,
Love, and Work.* New York: Dell.
Another very popular personality type book, that deals more explicitly with the 16 popular types of personalities.

Martin, Neil G. (2006). *Human Neuropsychology.* Essex: Prentice Hall Europe.
A neuropsych textbook suitable for undergraduates. Exactly what you might expect from a textbook.

Miller, James D. (2003). *Game Theory at Work.* New York: McGraw-Hill.
If you are not familiar with Game Theory, read this book. It provides simple, practical, real-life examples of strategic thinking and decision -making. Many examples will challenge your intuition and expand the way you see social expectations.

Morris, Desmond. (1984). *The Naked Ape.* New York: McGraw-Hill.
Morris was one of the first popular authors to openly describe humans as animals, even to the point of being condescending. He makes a good, simple argument for the idea of instinctual motivations.

O'Connor, Joseph & Seymour, John. (2002). *Introducing NLP.* London: Element.
This book has served as an introduction for decades of NLP practitioners and gives a good overview of the core ideas.

Pease, Alan. (1981). *Body Language.* North Sydney: Camel.
This is one of the most famous body language books ever, and is a good place to start if you want to know more about how body language works.

Ridley, Matt. (1994). *The Red Queen: Sex and the Evolution of Human Nature*. London: Penguin.
By examining plants and animals in nature, Matt Ridley provides an excellent, well-written point of view on our sexual behavior and why we do what we do.

Rowland, Ian. (2002). *The Full Facts Book of Cold Reading*. London: Ian Rowland, Ltd.
In my opinion this is the best cold reading book in existence. Unlike other books, Rowland actually details many real-life methods for telling fortunes, and is amazingly honest in doing so.

Sheehy, Gail. (2006). *Passages, Predictable Crises of Adult Life*. New York: Ballantine Books.
A brilliant examination of the life cycle of a typical adult.

Strauss, Neil. (2005) *The Game*. New York: Harper-Collins.
The book that launched the entire seduction community into the mainstream, many of their routines and methods are described during a highly engaging narrative.

Wroblewski, Luke. (2008). *Web Form Design, Filling in the Blanks*. New York: Rosenfeld.
A brilliant and simple book describing the fundamentals of designing web forms to maximize sales and registrations.

Trickshop.com. (2002). *Tradecraft, The Art and Science of Cold Reading*. Schaumburg: Trickshop.com, Inc.
Another excellent cold reading book, which relies on personality types to decide how to fine-tune the reading.

Webb, Kerin. (2008). *The Language Pattern Bible*. Dorset: Best Buddy Publishing.
A brick of a book that lists every hypnotic or deceptive language

pattern I have ever come across in 670 monotonous pages.

Enjoy these books, and I hope to hear from you online.

joelmarsh.com
thehipperelement.com
thecompositepersuasion.com

Made in the USA
Lexington, KY
26 November 2014